A
Book
Is a
Present

For Teresa with best wishes Margaret

Selecting Text for Intentional Teaching

Margaret E. Mooney

With a Foreword by Richard L. Allington, Ph.D.

Richard C. Owen Publishers, Inc.
Katonah, New York

Library of Congress Cataloging-in-Publication Data

Mooney, Margaret E.

    A book is a present : selecting texts for intentional teaching / Margaret E. Mooney; with a foreword by Richard Allington.

      p. cm.

    Includes bibliographical references and index.

    ISBN 1-57274-672-6 (pbk.)

    1. Children–Books and reading. 2. Reading. 3. Book selection. 4. Children's literature–Bibliography. I. Title.

Z1037.A1M79 2004

028.5'5–dc22
                                                      2004001107

Richard C. Owen Publishers, Inc.

PO Box 585

Katonah, NY 10536

914-232-3903; 914-232-3977 fax

www.RCOwen.com

Printed in the United States of America

9 8 7 6 5 4 3 2 1

Dedication

For Rosalie, who taught me how to look at books with new eyes.

MEM

Table of Contents

Teachers are invited to make photocopies of the bookmark at the end of this book for classroom use.

Foreword

Every now and then I'll pick up a book and wonder, "Why didn't I think of that?"

Margaret Mooney's small book is just that sort of text. In one source she has provided a virtual compendium of those features of texts that we seem often simply to take for granted. And in taking them for granted we may underestimate the complexity that texts can create for readers, for emerging readers especially.

But while this book draws our attention to these common but overlooked features of different sorts of texts, Mooney is quite clear that the text itself is but one of three aspects of a literacy lesson. She argues that first teachers must know their students. Know them well as developing readers and writers. Know their interests and preferences as well as how far they have traveled along the literacy continuum. Second, teachers must know the curriculum. Know what things are important to teach. What sort of proficiencies is the appropriate focus of the instruction? Then third, teachers must know the texts that children will experience. It is this third focus that is the primary topic of this text.

Mooney provides a new set of eyes for knowing the texts that students encounter. Knowing the texts means that a range of opportunities for teaching open up. Opportunities that support students as they work through texts. Opportunities that result in more children learning to manage increasingly complex texts. Opportunities to assist children as they ponder and explore how texts accomplish so many and varied things.

Mooney reminds us that for too long guided reading lessons have overemphasized fictional narratives and underemphasized different kinds of texts, including maps, directions, magazines, and, of course, informational texts (including traditional content area textbooks). She sets out in a straightforward manner the sorts of features that differentiate different types of texts. Along the way she discusses features that are common to all texts (e.g., fonts and type size), but features that are too often not explained to children.

She argues that in thinking about the texts to be used in instruction we need to remember that the key issue is "not what I can use the book to teach. . .but what the book offers the reader in terms of content, understanding about texts, and the role of the reader. . ." As she walks us through a variety of texts, she illustrates just this way of thinking about instructional opportunities.

My hunch is that this book is a good candidate for an annual rereading, just before the school year begins anew. It will continue to remind us of the breadth of instructional possibilities with most any text. It will remind us that good teaching doesn't assume anything. Remind us of the power we hold as teachers in developing children who can and do, joyously and voluntarily, read and write.

Richard L. Allington, Ph.D.
University of Florida

Introduction

About This Book

This is not a book about the teaching of reading, but rather a book for teachers of reading. Whether a certain program is mandated or whether teachers have the privilege and responsibility for selecting materials for use in their class reading program, knowing how to determine a text's complexity and how to select the most appropriate resources is critical. The premise underpinning this publication is that we can only make informed choices about which resource to use and how to present it when we know what the selection offers. We are then able to match a book to a student rather than try to manipulate a student's learning or skills to cope with a text unsuited to his or her capabilities, because either it is too easy or it presents so many challenges that the amount of intervention required takes away ownership of the reading and learning.

Knowing how to consider the textual and illustrative features of a book enables the teacher to identify those that would encourage application of strategies and skills that are secure within each learner, those that would offer practice of skills and strategies currently being acquired, and those that would present an achievable challenge. Considering the number of features in this way assists the teacher to make a decision not only about the book's suitability for that student or group of students but also about the most appropriate amount and nature of support that will ensure successful learning. In other words, knowing the learner and knowing the book are prerequisites to determining the most suitable instructional approach for introducing the book.

Labeling a book as suitable for an approach, whether it be read to, shared, guided, or independent; "to, with, or by;" or another set of names distinguishing the focus, is purely a starting point. It is likely that the approach used to introduce the book may change during the lesson as the teacher monitors each student's level of comprehension and fluency or decoding of unfamiliar vocabulary.

I have tried to explain some of the ways I look at books as a teacher and as a fledgling author of material for students and for teachers. Although not all of the ideas are written in first person, it is a personal view. I trust my passion for providing the best possible book for the teaching of reading does not override the practicalities and the realities of the classroom. I hope my writing confirms how much you know about books but may have let slip from the "front burner." I also hope it may trigger some new thoughts, thus making the reading worthwhile at more than the superficial level. Helping teachers help students, at any and all levels, read beyond the surface is the ultimate goal of my efforts in this publication.

The book comprises two main sections. In the first part, "Finding the Present," I share my understandings about various aspects and features of books, and how these support readers and writers. The second half, "Using the Present," details the features of a range of texts and offers suggestions for how they might be presented to readers and writers. Two of these titles, *The Birds at My Barn* and *Minibeasts,* are shrink-wrapped for use with this book. My writing about these books or any other examples included in the book does not endorse a specific level of suitability. The teacher knows the competence, experiences, and interests that the students bring to a book at a particular time, and that must underpin all decisions about selecting and presenting material.

Part I: *Finding the Present*

Cool
by Steven Morse
illustrated by Susan Banta

Chickens
by Rhonda Cox

HOKETICHEE
AND
THE MANATEE
by Kathleen...

Watermelon
by Rhonda Cox

Too
Many
Animals
Written by Frances Lee
Illustrated by Jane Wallace-Mitchell
alphakids

A Family of Beavers
by Marjorie Jackson
illustrated by Gay W. Holland

Chapter 1

Leveling— By Whom and for Whom

The identification of the perceived difficulty level of a text has long been an important development and marketing component of material designed for the teaching of reading. In the past, teachers have seldom questioned the formula that decreed a book suitable for a particular level or grade, although they may have struggled to ensure that all students were able to complete the associated activities suggested in the teacher's manuals. Graded material formed the core of the program, with supplementary material often being selected for its link to a thematic unit, because of a colleague's recommendation or simply because the book was appealing in some way. Under this pattern, students were often expected to fit the curriculum or program.

But now there is more talk about books being matched to the students and more questioning of the validity of levels. Almost every book bearing the educational label carries a level, although few include any explanation as to how the level was assigned, and certainly fewer include a description of the teaching style or student population of field trials to test the level before publication. Some teachers' manuals or resource guides include a statement that the assigned level is to be considered as a suggestion only, and a few include the probable supports and challenges appropriate for a particular stage of development. However, in most cases, teachers are left with insufficient knowledge about details of the determinants of the leveling, and they follow the levels with relatively little adjustment for their students' interests, experiences, cultural perspectives, and competencies.

Many levels are assigned by a combination of or all of the following: the introduction and repetition of basic vocabulary or words that can be decoded by applying certain phonological rules or patterns; the number of words, lines, or sentences on a page; the text-illustration match; and the perceived relevance of the content. While all these may be very important considerations, they barely skim the surface of the factors that contribute to a text's complexity.

The list of text and illustrative elements included in this chapter does not constitute a definitive or exclusive checklist. A predetermined number assigned to a book does not determine whether a text is suitable for a particular grade or group of students. The list is included here to show the range of factors that can contribute to the way a book provides challenges and supports. Teachers need to continually remind themselves that what may be a challenge for one student or group of students may be a support for others. Knowing how to review a book and determine its relevance for the competencies, background experiences and knowledge, and interests of the students is a prerequisite for the selection of any material for a classroom. Only then can teachers make an appropriate decision about accepting or amending the assigned or suggested level of a particular text for a particular group of students at a particular time for use in a particular approach.

> **Approach –** *amount and nature of support and instruction to cause engagement with a task.*

The following factors contribute to the difficulty level of a book. They are discussed in more detail in the remainder of the book but are included here as a reminder of the complexity of pre-assigning a level to a book or perhaps the foolishness of blindly following that pre-assigned level without reviewing the book in detail.

Cover

Title

What perspective does the title set?

Does it reveal the punch line, provide a clue to the most advantageous reading style, present a perspective, or indicate the theme or the topic of the work?

Cover Illustration

Does the illustration on the cover match or reflect the title?

Does the illustration portray action (perhaps an incident) or mood or introduce a character or subject?

Does the illustration give a clue about the author's perspective or indicate reading style?

Blurb

What does it introduce to the reader?

Is it all "teaser," or does it introduce content and perspective?

Does it include author information, especially about other books that might be familiar to the intended reader?

What is credible once the marketing content has been removed?

Title Page

If there is an illustration on the title page, does it enable confirmation of some of the predictions made from the cover?

What extra information can be gleaned from the illustration on the title page?

Table of Contents

If the table of contents is annotated, is it clear which are chapter headings and which is supplementary explanation?

Are the page numbers easy to match with the title in the table of contents?

Are the chapter headings explanatory, teaser, or simply numerical?

If the book is informational, is there sufficient detail for readers to plan their reading?

Content

What previous knowledge of the topic does it assume the reader has?

How relevant is the topic, theme, or issue?

Does the author make clear which of these should claim priority in the reading?

Is the content and perspective credible for the intended reader?

Is the main content presented in the illustrations or visuals?

Does the content avoid dilution or distortion of information that would require unlearning at a later stage of development?

Is the content devoid of didacticism or moralistic writing that clouds the theme or issue?

Does the textual or illustrative content avoid stereotyping any group or activity?

Does the content meet the expectations engendered by the information on the cover?

How many characters or subjects are introduced? When? How?

Do the characters change dramatically during the work?

Are the characters credible?

Is the main idea or theme accessible or influenced by too many time or scene changes?

Does the story line or main information rely on illustrations, or can the text stand alone?

Does the text have an identifiable shape to support the reader?

Is the new information introduced in accessible chunks and with acceptable pacing?

Are there appropriate transitions linking incidents or sections of information?

Form[1]

Is the form or genre suitable for the content and the author's perspective?

Are the usual conventions of the form followed?

Is the illustrative material appropriate for the form?

Language

Does the language suit the topic, theme, form, and writer's style?

How much language will be easily decodable by the intended reader?

How much content-specific language, context-specific language, cultural-specific language, or dialectal language is included? Is it explained within the text, or is there an accessible glossary?

How often is "new" vocabulary repeated?

Is the tense consistent?

What is the balance of book and natural language and of direct and indirect speech?

What figures of speech are used?

Is there sufficient redundancy in the text to aid fluency, or is there an absence of basic vocabulary linking essential ideas?

Are there too many low-imagery words in succession that have no discernible meaning?

---

[1] For further information on text forms and features, see: Mooney, Margaret E. 2001. *Text Forms and Features: A Resource for Intentional Teaching.* Katonah, NY: Richard C. Owen Publishers, Inc.

Do the pronouns have referent nouns?

Is there an overdose of nonsensical vocabulary detracting from the real content or message?

Does the range of sentence structures support or reduce the impact of the content?

Style

Is the writing style appropriate for the content, form, and intended reader?

Does the writer maintain a consistent style?

Does the writing style avoid condescension?

Illustrative Material

Does the illustrative material reflect, extend, or present another view of the content and its focus?

Does the illustrative material complement or dominate the text?

Are the illustrations appropriate for the intended focus and for the characters or subject?

Is the illustrative material placed before, after, or near the relevant text?

Is the range of illustrative material appropriate for the content, form, and intended reader?

Do the illustrations complement the author's style?

Typography

Is there a satisfactory balance of text, space, and illustrative material?

Is there a clear reading path?

Is the typeface appropriate in size, style, and spacing?

Are normal print conventions followed?

Is the text clear of all margins, leaving room for holding the book without covering text?

Is the text laid out in manageable chunks?

Are the features of the form followed?

Is the paper of sufficient weight to avoid show-through?

Is the book easy to hold?

Is the placement of supplementary material (e.g., footnotes) appropriate?

It is not intended that the aforementioned list should be worked through with any one book. And it is certainly not intended to be used to scrutinize levels already assigned to books. It is included as a reminder of some of the elements that cause the content of one book to be more accessible than another. However, the degree to which that plays out is dependent on the reader's competencies and understanding of the purpose of the reading and commitment to working to engage in meaningful dialogue with the author.

Knowing what a book offers is only useful information when it is matched to the reader, and that is the responsibility and privilege of the classroom teacher. The remainder of this book provides examples of how the framework included in this chapter can assist in that matching.

Chapter 2

What Kind of Book Is It?

One of the first distinctions, although often not the easiest to make, is whether a book is fiction or nonfiction. Fiction is generally described as works of imagination in which the content is feigned or fabricated. Nonfiction is generally described as offering opinions or conjectures based on fact. However, the widely accepted view of the latter as opinion or conjecture based on fact does not really stand-up to such a simplistic distinction, because books on diets, how to become a millionaire overnight, poetry, and fairy tales are housed in the nonfiction section of the library. Although within the class setting the distinction made between fiction and nonfiction is often simply what is not true and what is true, I prefer to talk about fiction and informational texts. By using the term informational, I am reminding the reader of the main purpose of reading nonfiction, which is to search for or select information. Nell Duke, in *Reading Research Quarterly* (2000, 205), defines informational text as "texts and contexts having many or all of the following features:

(a) A function to communicate information about the natural or social world, typically from one presumed to be more knowledgeable on the subject to one presumed to be less so;

(b) An expectation of durable factual content;

(c) Timeless verb constructions;

(d) Generic noun constructions;

(e) Technical vocabulary;

(f) Classificatory and definitional material;

(g) Comparative/contrastive, problem/solution, cause/effect, or like text structures;

(h) Frequent repetition of the topical theme;

(i) Graphical elements such as diagrams, indices, page numbers, and maps."

Genre—*classification of text forms and structures.*

Whether one chooses to use the label nonfiction or informational text, there are major differences in the focus and usually in the layout and features of fiction and informational works. These differences often require different reading styles, such as browsing, skimming to pick up the general gist of a piece, scanning to locate a certain word or item of information, researching to select or validate details, or close reading to attend to all details and to understand the author's intent. The differences of focus and layout also influence the purposes for reading as well as the outcomes.

When reading fiction, the focus is on the plot and how it is carried forward. When reading informational text, the focus is on the information and how it is presented.

As long as the fiction is within the realm of credibility, the content is seldom questioned. However, the validity of the information is often of major concern. This means the author is often able to substantiate the facts with references, research data, or specific examples.

A piece of fiction is usually dependent on the sum and sequence of the parts. The chapters usually end at a high point, with a hint of what is to come, encouraging the reader to continue reading. The parts of an informational piece are often complete in themselves, although they are linked to and/or support the central idea or theme. Each chapter may end with a concluding or summary statement or paragraph. The chapters do not necessarily need to be read in sequence, which means a clear table of contents is more critical in an informational text than in one of fiction.

The title and chapter headings in a piece of fiction are more likely to be teasers than in an informational text, where they often indicate the author's perspective or the detail of the content. The illustrations in a work of fiction (especially that in material beyond the early stages of reading development) often portray mood or encapsulate one incident or part thereof, and they are usually created specifically for that piece. Informational texts may include a range of illustrative material, some of which may have been obtained from other publications or sources, which means there will be a longer acknowledgment or permissions section than in most works of fiction. Illustrated anthologies in fiction may be the exception. Unless the informational text includes an interview or a large number of direct quotes, the bulk of the information and action will be descriptive text, whereas direct speech may form a large part of a piece of fiction, especially a novel.

Although the text forms may often differ between those generally classified as fiction and those usually labeled informational or nonfiction, there may be some similarities in the underlying structure. For example, many novels are based on a problem and solution or series of problems and solutions, which is also common in informational texts. Both kinds of texts may have a foundation built on comparing and contrasting. In the case of fiction, this may be through the antagonist and protagonist, whereas in informational text it may be the way the workings of two governments are presented. Cause-and-effect is a common structure in both text types.

Other commonalties of structure lie in the way the readers are supported through the text. For example, a sequential or chronological structure is as common in fiction as in informational text. The cyclic, cumulative (as in *The House That Jack Built*), and interlocking structure (as in *Brown Bear, Brown Bear, What Do You See?*, Martin Jr 1992) that often form the structure of a fiction text at the early levels are also common in informational text. For example, the food chain of animals and insects is sometimes used in texts of interlocking structure or the flow of water in a cumulative text.

Much time and effort have been expended in trying to determine definitive descriptors of various text forms. This discussion has heightened our understanding of the different forms of writing and of our expectations of students' ability to "twist the pen" to write in a wide range of text forms. One of the wake-up calls I experienced as a result of that prolonged discussion was how we need to ensure that students have experience in viewing, hearing, and reading the forms of text that we expect them to write. This exposure and practice needs to be as intentional and focused as that for the most favorite story, while the support and guidance given in writing needs to match that given in the composition of a narrative. Using fiction and nonfiction text for instructional purposes requires familiarity with the intent and features of the different forms, because this information is critical when selecting a book for use or display in the classroom. There are many ways of classifying the various forms, but the following basic list is presented as a reminder of some of the forms commonly used as prompts for students' writing and is therefore a guide for selecting resources. Details of features for each of the forms can be found in other publications, including *Text Forms and Features* (Mooney 2001).

Common Forms

Fiction

Narrative: to entertain, to comfort, to sustain, to delight, to activate imagination, to extend experiences and understandings vicariously

Includes novels, ballads, epics, short stories, fictitious biographies and travelogues, traditional tales, folk tales, fables, myths, legends, letters, diaries, mysteries, romances, farce, fantasy fiction, science fiction, historical fiction . . .

Structures include cumulative or diminishing, interlocking, sequential, cyclic, episodic, or alternating events (as in good event, bad event, good . . .)

Poetry, verse, and rhyme: to entertain, to cause thought and reflection, to create images, to humor, to comfort

Includes poems, haiku, limericks, sonnets, epics, ballads, finger and number rhymes, songs, cinquains . . .

Plays: to present for the entertainment or education of others, to impersonate

Includes monologues, sketches, comedy, tragedy . . .

Informational Texts

Expository: To explain, to detail, to systematically describe or present a case

Includes biographies, autobiographies, business letters, diaries, journals, memoirs, articles, reports, reviews, almanacs, encyclopedias . . .

Persuasive: To change attitude, to get "buy-in"

Includes brochures, letters to the editor, editorials, posters, advertisements, debates, speeches, business letters . . .

Procedural: To detail a sequence and method

Includes recipes, directions, instructions, manuals, plans . . .

Transactional: To engender a response, to detail two-way communication

Includes debates, interviews, correspondence, memos . . .

Whatever the book, structure, or content, the key questions when selecting a book should be, "How will this book help these students know more about how words work, how language works, how texts work, and how reading works? What amount and kind of support will I need to provide to ensure the students are successful at gaining and using the information and ideas for and by themselves?"

I use the words "gain and use ideas and information" to replace the often-quoted "gain meaning" because I believe that using what we learn as we read is what provides the intrinsic rewards for the learners. If students become reliant on extrinsic feedback such as words of praise or rewards, reading will not become a self-sustaining and self-motivating pursuit but rather a task to gain commendation. Teachers must help students understand that learning requires effort and that effort brings its own satisfaction and rewards. It is important to keep the intrinsic benefits of reading in mind when considering what a book offers, because it is not what the book can be used to teach that is important, but rather what the book offers the reader in terms of content, understanding about texts, and the role of being a reader.

I also use the words "gain and use ideas and information" as central to my longer explanation of reading and writing because it applies to instruction and assessment as well as to selecting a book.

- When reading to be entertained, to find comfort, or to lose ourselves in another world, we gain and use ideas and information to comprehend why we are as we are and to know more about our real and imaginary worlds and the real and imaginary worlds of others.

- When reading history, we gain and use ideas and information to find out why and how people act as they do or have done in our world and in the world of others, and what that means for us today.

- When reading science, we gain and use ideas and information to know why and how things are as they are or change as they do in the natural and physical world.

- When reading mathematics, we gain and use ideas and information to know why and how things can be quantified and represented in a number of codes.

- When reading music, we gain and use ideas and information to know why and how we can create tunes and sounds in a particular pattern.

These understandings also apply to writing. For example, when writing a history report, we use and share our ideas and information to know why and how people thought and acted as they did and what it means for us today.

A well-chosen book will leave students with a residue of learning about their world and the wider world and also a deeper conviction that reading is a manageable and worthwhile activity. The new learning and the greater understanding of the benefits of reading and of learning itself form a springboard for further explorations through the printed word.

Chapter 3

Supports and Challenges

Even for skilled readers, every reading brings supports and challenges, although we are usually unaware that we are meeting complexities that require application of particular skills and strategies. Every time we view or read text, our understandings about reading and about what is read are either confirmed or amended in some way. The degree to which we are aware of that confirmation or amendment is usually unnoticed. However, on other occasions we are conscious of needing to reread for clarification or understanding, of seeking familiar parts of a word, or scanning for vowels to break the word into syllables to see if the word is in our aural vocabulary.

Instruction—guiding the learner through the supports and challenges of experiences necessary to acquire and practice new understandings and skills leading to independent application.

Beginning readers, fluent readers coping with text unfamiliar in content or form, and those struggling with material that lacks immediate relevance are undoubtedly more aware of the challenges than the supports. One of our key tasks as teachers is to know how to select and consider the most appropriate approach to ensure students understand how authors and illustrators support readers. Once students know the supportive techniques that authors embed in a text, we can then help them use that knowledge to overcome challenges with confidence. Students need to expect that there will be some challenge in much of the material they meet during a school day and that those challenges will bring some discomfort within as they work through the difficulties. Learning does not take place without such a moment of being on the brink of the known and unknown. It is at that moment of "I think I know; oh, yes, I know" that learning occurs. Our task in instruction is to take each student to the brink of the safety of the known and to give a gentle nudge into the safety of the unknown without the student fearing failure or frustration. The material we select becomes the vehicle for us to help students make the step into the unknown successfully. To select material that enables us to show this through explanation, sufficient guidance, and practice for that skill or strategy to become an integral part of the student's repertoire, we need to know how the book will support or challenge each reader in our care. We need to know our students as readers and writers, not only what they can and do achieve but also their potential and the influences on their learning and knowledge.

All students bring years of living, loving, and learning to their current learning opportunities and challenges. Whatever those years have brought their way in terms of experiences or nurturing, full-strength emotions have been at work. There are huge implications for the material we select. If the printed word is to be its own magnet showing the benefits of reading and drawing readers back to revisit a text, the content must reflect the ups and downs of life, the way people react and interact, and the way people cope with a wide range of situations. And the reality of the content must not be diluted beyond what we would hope the students would include in their own writing.

We need to know the range of language registers the students bring, such as how they communicate on the playground; the language they hear when their families congregate to celebrate, mourn, or worship; the structures they hear in the course of family life; the cadence and vocabulary of stories read at home or preschool; and the talk of their imaginative play. Each of these registers will influence their expectations and comprehension of the printed word.

Students' previous experiences with books will also influence the way we select material to continue their literacy journey. If, for example, the books have been predominantly texts of a repeated pattern, it may be time to introduce more varied structures. Or, if they have had a diet of chapter books or novels, the new selection should include some shorter texts of more varied genre, including some informational texts. If our students think of reading as struggling to keep up with the class reading of a text that is always followed by a written activity of literal comprehension questions, their horizons could be broadened through books that encourage reading and thought beyond the text or books that engender an oral or more creative response.

Similarly, their previous experiences with learning and instruction influence how they approach, read, and respond to books in ways other than just the decoding or comprehending. If previous instruction in skills has been isolated from, or prior to, the reading of the text, students may have difficulty when they meet challenges while reading. Students who have been taught skills in context and view meeting challenges as part of reading see overcoming challenges as part of the nature and joy of being a reader. If the students have not had continuous access to choosing books for their own enjoyment or do not practice new learning independently, the current selection would need to be an easy read with just a few challenges to develop confidence in reading unfamiliar text independently.

Other considerations beyond a pre-assigned level include those relating to culture. Imagination and values are shaped by cultural heritage. What is reality for one student may be imaginable fantasy for another. Another student may not be able to relate to the content or humor in any way or to accept the values or behavior the author presents as acceptable. An incident within a book that causes offense can taint the way the whole book is viewed.

> **Skill**—*an appropriate and practiced way of doing something.*
> **Strategy**—*a pattern of thinking and application to accomplish a task. A strategy is usually a combination of skills.*

As school populations became more diverse and the public more demanding of cultural awareness, there was a swing toward publishing more culturally specific material to address these issues. However, in recent years, some of this cultural-specific material has been lost as more publishers have produced material for the world market. Efforts to try to meet the needs of a number of markets have sometimes made the material more general—for example, not listing a specific location or using cartoon-type illustrations to avoid denoting a particular culture or race.

Range of Readers

Seeking material that does enable students to identify with characters, settings, customs, and values while at the same time being aware of the idea that "supports for one may be challenges for another" should remain a high priority in the selection of material. The notion of "supports for one—challenge for another" also applies to the range of learning styles, attitudes, and competencies of the students within any group. Three groups of readers comprise most classrooms, and these groups could be described as passionate, functional, and struggling.

Passionate Readers

Passionate readers make time to read, often at the expense of completing assigned tasks. They read anywhere and are often oblivious

> ***Learning styles**—the ways in which new learning is acquired, for example, visually, or slowly accruing through frequent practice, or by shadowing or copying more knowledgeable others.*

to what is going on around them or to people talking to them. They seek out new books, are able to find and talk about their favorites, and will often draw others to look at a particular illustration. They usually read quickly, with some needing to be encouraged to read at a slower pace to fully comprehend the text. Passionate readers are usually able to select a book quickly when necessary, but they also enjoy "dipping and delving" when time allows a more leisurely perusal. Some students labeled as passionate are really only enthusiastic about a particular kind of book or a specific topic. The selection of books for passionate readers should include those that deepen their understandings about reading and broaden their reading interests and habits rather than solely address the issue of difficulty and reaching higher levels with great speed. Books for these students should encourage them to savor the delights of reading and of what is read.

Functional Readers

The bulk of readers in most classes are considered to be in the group labeled as functional readers. These are students who work diligently to meet extrinsic requirements and who know that reading is a worthwhile activity but who are not passionate enough to put all else aside to read independently or allow themselves to be "lost in a book" on a regular basis. They approach unfamiliar text with an expectation of meeting and being able to overcome challenges but do not face these with enthusiasm. Readers labeled functional are usually competent comprehending at the literal (understanding content as stated by the author) and inferential (thinking beyond the text) levels but often require prompting to think analytically as they consider the effectiveness of the text and consider the craft of the writer and the reader.

Responses to text usually indicate some internalization of content but often do not extend to creative extension or prolonged thought after the reading has been completed. These students are usually on task; in other words, they usually complete reading assignments and are usually attentive in class, group, and individual reading activities. Although they may form the bulk of the class, functional readers are often the forgotten group when it comes to book selection. Teachers are anxious to keep the passionate readers busy and their interests satisfied, or they are preoccupied with helping to find material manageable for the struggling readers, leaving the group of willing but only partially motivated functional readers to either select from the books that are too challenging or to select those that provide little or no challenge. Yet these students are equally deserving of having access to material to "light their reading fires" rather than merely "fill their vase."

Struggling Readers

The term "struggling readers" in this book is used generically for students who are discouraged, overwhelmed, or confused about their role as readers. They have difficulty understanding and applying the skills and strategies to turn the squiggles and codes on the page into meaningful thoughts and information. These students often struggle to articulate their understandings about what they read, whether responding orally, in writing, or visually. Even if these students had access to the widest range of material, many of them would choose inappropriately, not know how to choose, or want to keep making new choices. If the choice held interest, it might be for the illustrative material, and it is likely that it would be informational text that would be viewed or would be suitable for browsing, with the text probably too challenging for close or detailed reading.

Many of these students perceive any "school" reading as too difficult and have learned avoidance tactics, especially if there is an expectation that they will read aloud or will be required to complete a related assignment. Yet these same students can often interpret very complex diagrams or provide intricate details gleaned from tables on the sports page. In some cases, their effort is commensurate with the intrinsic rewards to satisfy their interests. In other cases, they are able to read figures and illustrative material but unable to decode connected text at a sufficient pace to comprehend.

Texts suitable for these students should avoid condescension in structure or content and should have immediate interest appeal. When the students browse through the books, they should be able to make immediate connections, enticing them to take a closer look and engage in meaningful dialogue with the author as well as the illustrator. The characters should not give a sense that the book was intended for younger readers. The language should be clear, avoiding a succession of pronouns, low-imagery words (for example, "it could be said that it would still be as it was even if he had come earlier"), nonsensical words (for example, "a senny, sanny, sunny day"), or words with multiple meanings ("he saw the bear through the woods"). Students who are discouraged or overwhelmed or confused about reading need access to books of the highest quality—books that act as a magnet, not only drawing readers back for repeated readings but also having the power to attract readers to explore other books.

I remember a conversation during my first meeting with a sixth-grade student whom I had been asked to help. The bookmark in his current instructional text read, "A book is a present you give yourself every time you open it." The bookmark was obviously new or unused, so I asked if it was a recent gift or if it was something he had chosen. He answered, "Nope. I don't actually believe it. It's only a present if you can read it. The teacher put it there. I guess she was trying to . . . well, kid me along."

There can be no kidding when it comes to matching books to readers.

Chapter 4

A Book Is a Present...

What is it about a book that makes it " . . . a present you can give yourself every time you open it?" What is a present for one may not be a present for another, and what makes it a present at one time may not have the same appeal every time the book is opened. Yet the appeal usually lingers, causing subsequent revisiting and enjoyment. There is no definitive list of essential traits, but some of the presents that books offer are outlined in the remainder of this chapter.

A good book has something worthwhile to say to and with you. You feel as if the author has chosen you, not only as the prime audience but also as the lead conversationalist, trusting you to contribute your ideas and knowledge as you weave your thoughts in and out of the printed word. This affinity with the author allows you to feel at ease with yourself, even when you encounter some moments of wonderment or are transported to a new comfort zone. As you relax into the reading, it is sometimes difficult to know who has the pen in hand, because you find yourself writing along with the author. You barely notice when the author is leading you to a new vista; then, all of a sudden, it is there.

You are transported into a new world. It has been crafted with such credibility that you are excited to be exploring ideas or information that you had never thought about or perhaps did not even realize you had the capacity to think about. You find that what had previously seemed out of your reach is now part of your conscious thought, something you can easily handle and even control. The author has turned the densest into something palpable, the most obscure into something of clarity and immediate relevance, or the most heart-rending into something comprehensible. Whether it has come upon you by surprise or gradually and gently, you feel comfortable with the journey and want to mull it over, viewing it through a different lens to see other facets of the gem or bring new light onto what has been in the shadows.

The present of finding new views or being shown that there are more perspectives to explore leads to an intrinsic thirst for even more learning. This anticipation happens when the author challenges and supports you rather than makes demands. A challenge is like a teaser, an active conversation, but a demand is a one-way expectation. The author shepherds your thoughts and understandings rather than pulls you into a predetermined framework of acceptable viewpoints. Once a new view or level of understanding has been explored, the author of a good book draws you back to discover even more depths or to reflect on your previous journey. What was it that signaled that door to new thought or new learning? You may have been nudged into reflecting on your affinity with the language and the way it was expressed, or your interest may have been captivated to such a degree that you want to experiment with or test new understandings or knowledge against what you previously thought was the "last word." Or you may simply want to try to relive the moment of going from the known to the unknown to accommodate and enjoy the moments of being confident in what you now know.

But a good book encourages you to think not only about what you know but also about what you feel, and to remind you that it is acceptable to feel that way and that someone else understands. A good book affords solace. It brings comfort. It matches and supplies our very need at that moment. It holds a mirror up to our musings, enabling us to see them for what they are and what could be, all the while accepting them but also showing us the next door to richer understandings about ourselves, our worlds, and the worlds of others.

A good book supports your understanding of yourself not only within these worlds but also within your life as a reader. The author allows you to create your own pace for the conversation while also providing subtle signals when your participation in the conversation seems urgent or when the author wants to reflect with you. The flow of information or the story line has sufficient strength and clarity that you can quickly regain your place after leaving the text for a period of time.

Finishing a good book is as exciting as beginning one. Any thoughts of sadness at knowing the last word has been lifted off the page are replaced by the anticipation of continuing the thoughts that the author has stirred or rekindled within us. Chunks of language come rolling back, sometimes flowing off our tongue, for we have internalized them to such a degree that we know them beyond knowing. Visions of incidents or scenes portrayed in word and image flood into our imaginations, allowing us to vicariously restage a memorable moment or assume a character's role as if preparing for the real life version of what the author has helped you create.

What makes a good book for skilled readers works for books for students of all levels and competencies. It is not what the book teaches that matters, but rather what the book leaves as a residue within the reader. Margaret Meek, writing in *Learning to Read* (1982, 20-21), describes the teaching role of the text in this way:

> *In the act of reading what someone has written, we enter into a kind of social relationship with the writer who has something to tell us or something to make with words and language. The reader takes on this relationship, which may feel like listening, but is in fact different in that it is more active. He recreates the meaning by processing the text at his own speed and in his own way. As he brings the text to*

life, he casts back and forth in his head for connections between what he is reading and what he already knows. He pauses, rushes on, selects from his memory whatever relates the meaning to his experience or his earlier reading, in a rich and complex to-ing and fro-ing in his head, storing, reworking, understanding or being puzzled. Some successful readers say that they feel they are helping to create the work with *the author. Children talk about being* in *a book, as if that were a place. We know we can possess a book in our heads after the actual volume has been returned to the library. Sometimes we carry phrases and characters about with us for the rest of our lives. Later we read significant things that illumine texts we had read before we left school. We gain more lives than one, more memories than we ever could have from what happened to us; in fact, a whole alternative existence, in our own culture and that of others. This is what the learner has to learn to do, and what we expect teachers to teach. Literacy has powerful consequences, not the least is that it changes one's view of oneself and the world.*

Chapter 5

At First Glance

The cover of a book usually reveals much more than a few clues to what the book may be about. Indeed, if books being selected for the teaching of reading are viewed only in this light, the focus of the lesson is likely to remain at a surface level rather than promoting deeper understandings about the act of reading. In any reading within an educational setting, there needs to be a balance of what is read and how it is read. The viewing of the cover and introductory pages of a book should include what information or clues there are about the probable content, how it will be presented, and what will be the best way to access it. As teachers match this information with what they know about the students' competencies, previous reading experiences, and interests, the focus will remain on the students' role as the decoders and interpreters of the ideas and information presented through text and illustrative material.

The front and back covers, title page, introductory pages, table of contents, and inside covers of almost all books provide a range of helpful information to assist the reader to make likely predictions about these elements of the proposed reading. Gleaning information beyond the content takes any connotation of prediction as being simply guessing to "eliminating the alternatives" or considering the most likely path for the reading.

> **Reading styles –** *ways in which a reader changes pace and attention to detail in response to the text or to accommodate a specific purpose for the reading. Browsing, skimming, scanning, rereading, and close reading are examples of reading styles.*

Information able to be gleaned from the covers and introductory material may include the title and whether the book has a sole or multiple authors, is a compilation of works, or is an edited selection. If other work by the author or some of the authors is familiar, there will be an expectation of style and perhaps writing form. If more than one author is listed, it is an immediate signal that more than one view will be presented, thus requiring the readers to compare and contrast and synthesize ideas or information. If the book is an edited collection, it is possible that there will be conflicting opinions selected to encourage reflective thought within the readers.

The title often indicates more than the topic. For example, the title *Raving about Rainforests* (Marcus 2002) indicates both the topic and the bias, signaling to the readers that they will likely meet persuasive language or information focused on a particular perspective.

Other titles, such as C. S. Lewis's *The Lion, the Witch, and the Wardrobe* (originally published in 1950), indicate main characters but leave an air of mystery about the way these will be portrayed. Some texts, particularly those in the fables, myths, and legends genres, signal the problem-and-solution structure of the work. Examples include the Aesop's fables, "How the Tortoise Got Its Shell" and "Why the Ant Is a Thief." A piece entitled "How to Make a Delicious Dessert for a Day in the Desert" helps the reader prepare for a procedural text in recipe format describing a very specific type of dessert. The only mystery may be what such a dessert could look like or its ingredients, but there is a clear framework of how the information is most likely to be presented.

And Then There Were Birds

A Native American Tale
retold by Casey Lynn Allen
pictures by Gregory G. Newson

Figure 5.1: Front cover of *And Then There Were Birds*

Subtitles or extra information about the title and/or author also help the reader anticipate the probable form and focus of the writing. As shown in Figure 5.1, the words "A Native American Tale" and "retold by . . ." provide the setting and indicate that the text is likely to be culturally specific, the original story line may be familiar, and the structure is likely to follow the form of a traditional tale. When this latter feature is considered with the title, which indicates nature and the creation of something, there is an extra clue that the piece is likely to be a myth. (This prediction can be confirmed on the inside front cover, as shown in Figure 5.2.)

To my mother and husband with love — the author

Myth

A myth is a make-believe tale that people in a certain culture tell to explain something about nature or creation. Often the character in the myth responsible for the magical happening is a supernatural or spiritual being. *And Then There Were Birds* is a retelling of a native American myth about the creation of birds.

Books for Young Learners

Text copyright © 2000 by Casey Lynn Allen
Illustrations copyright © 2000 by Gregory G. Newson

All rights reserved.

No part of this publication may be reproduced or transmitted in any form or by any means, electronic or mechanical, including photocopying, recording, or any information storage and retrieval system, without permission in writing from the publisher.

Richard C. Owen Publishers, Inc.
PO Box 585
Katonah, New York 10536

Summary: A retelling of a native American tale about the creation of birds.

ISBN 1-57274-284-4

Color separations by Leo P. Callahan, Inc., Binghamton, New York

Printed in the United States of America

9 8 7 6 5 4 3 2 1

Figure 5.2: Inside front cover of *And Then There Were Birds*

Covers of illustrated texts, especially those in the picture book category, include the illustrator's or photographer's name. As with the author's credit, familiarity with the person's work is likely to engender expectations that, in the case of the illustrator or photographer, can be confirmed by the front cover. Books written and illustrated, either with pictures or photographs, by the same person have special significance for students, because it is our expectation of them when they publish their work.

Figure 5.3: Cover of *Chickens*

The **Books for Young Learners**[1] collection includes several books written and illustrated with photographs by Rhonda Cox. The overprinting of the hand-drawn chickens on the cover photograph of *Chickens* (Cox 1997) shown in Figure 5.3 provides a contrast with the photograph of one chicken, giving a clear message to beginning readers to look at word endings to check for plurals.

---

[1]**Books for Young Learners** published by Richard C. Owen Publishers, Inc., Katonah, New York.

Figure 5.4: Cover of *Cool*

The cover illustration often portrays the mood or setting of the story, providing opportunity for introductory discussion to include prediction of the kind of vocabulary that might match that aspect of the book. For example, soft colors in the illustrations are often used for gentle stories or those dealing with emotions of sadness or solitude, or the illustrations might indicate characters or portray a key incident. Sometimes the illustration is a teaser, as on the cover of *Cool* (Morse 2001), shown in Figure 5.4, in which multiple meanings of the word "cool" are portrayed. The cover illustrations of many of the books designed primarily for the teaching of reading, and especially for beginning readers, show the punch line or climax of the story. In such cases, it may be wise to keep the introductory discussion brief, leaving the surprise of the story to be discovered in the course of reading the book. The cover illustration often has strong links to that on the title page.

Whereas the front cover of a book always carries similar information of title, author, and illustrator, the information on the back cover varies from book to book, series to series, and publisher to publisher. Information on the back cover may include blurbs, author and illustrator biographical information, suggested leveling, other titles in the series, illustrations, or endorsements or excerpts from

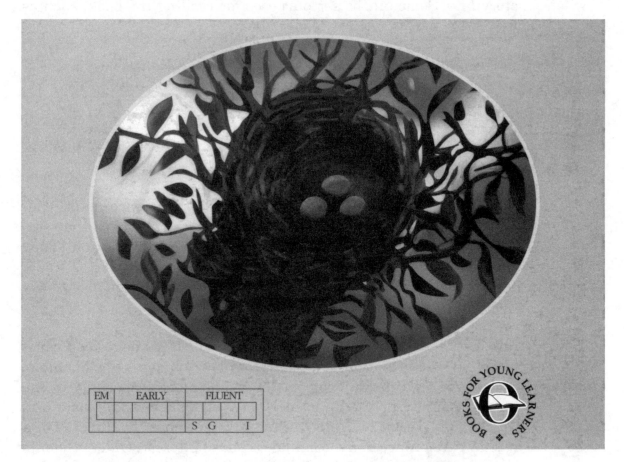

Figure 5.5: Back cover of *And Then There Were Birds*

reviews, or it may continue the wrap-around illustration from the front cover. Any and all of this information help readers think about how and what they can expect to read within the covers. The combination of the title, the bird-shape leaf, and the bird on the front cover and the illustration of birds' eggs in a nest in a tree on the back cover of *And Then There Were Birds* (Allen 2000) as shown in Figure 5.5 give hints about the story line and that events continue beyond the book. The blurb, usually written by an employee of the publisher, often gives more hints about the writing style from which the readers can get a feeling for the required reading style than telling about the content. The persuasive language may do no more than tease the reader or distort the focus of the information or the story line. Some blurbs set purposes for reading the book, such as for *Search and Discover* (Cooper 2002):

> *Whether you live in a big city or out in the country, you can learn about nature. All you have to do is look around you, ask questions, and observe. What could you learn from studying a tree or a tiny crab? Find out how two teenagers made big discoveries when they took a close look at plants and animals near their homes.*

Comments about the leveling of material for the teaching of reading have already been made. It is sufficient to say here that students' attention should not be drawn to this information. They should not see reading as a race, a sequence of set books or "readers," or a series of hoops one has to jump through to be able to say they are readers.

Publication data on the inside front cover or front pages can carry interesting information, especially to older readers. For example, the number of times a book has been published, especially in the case of classics, or the difference between the copyright date and that of publication indicates an author's patience. In the case of a retelling, reference to the original can be of interest. Older students should also understand the significance of copyright, both as the author's right to own material and the user's responsibility to seek permission, as included in the acknowledgment section. Dedications can remind students that authors write or illustrators draw and photograph with specific audiences in mind. Many adults tend to skip these publication data, yet that data remind students of the number of people contributing to the development and publication of a book and also of the similarity to their roles as authors when publishing their writing.

Cool

by Steven Morse
illustrated by Susan Banta

Richard C. Owen Publishers, Inc.
Katonah, New York

Figure 5.6: Title page of *Cool*

The title page is often seen as merely repeating the author and illustrator credits from the cover, but illustrations on the title page often offer other clues about the focus of what is to come. Sometimes one part of the cover illustration is brought into closer focus, as in *And Then There Were Birds,* in which the bird-shaped leaf from the front cover is repeated by itself. This myth tells how the Great Spirit turns leaves into birds. The illustration on the title page of *Cool* shown in Figure 5.6 opens up further options for thinking about the meanings of the word "cool," which is the focus of the book. Similarly, the three feathers on the title page of *The Birds at My Barn* (Moeller 2000) give a clue that the different birds presented in the text will provide opportunities for readers to make comparisons.

Some title pages, especially but not exclusively of informational texts or textbooks, introduce a subheading specifying the intended audience or providing more information about the content. For example, the cover reads *Which Native Tree?* (Crowe 1992) and the title page reads *Which Native Tree? A Simple Guide to the Identification of New Zealand Native Trees*, or the words *The Chicago Manual of Style: The 13th Edition of a Manual of Style Revised and Extended* (1998) appear on the cover, and the title page has an extra subheading of "For Authors, Editors, and Copywriters."

Contents

Flower Farm 2
Wheat Farm 6
Apple Orchard 10
Pumpkin Farm 16

Figure 5.7: Table of contents of *The Busy Harvest*

The table of contents is a listing of the contents or the author telling readers how the book is organized. The listing provides a brief overview of the sequence or, in the case of a narrative, perhaps of the story line, although this depends on whether the chapter titles are teasers or indicators of the way the plot might unfold. However, the table of contents has another and more important function, especially in the context of helping students to understand their roles as readers. The table of contents enables the readers to map their planned reading and decide the order in which the chapters are likely to satisfy their interest or aid the completion of their search for specific information. Annotated tables of contents are particularly helpful when specific information is sought. Other considerations include the proximity of the page numbers to the titles and the way the listing may give an indication if the text within chapters might follow a pattern. For example, the table of contents from *The Busy Harvest* (Mooney 2000) (see Figure 5.7) lists the first two chapters, "Flower Farm" and "Wheat Farm," as each being four pages, which signals they will probably have a similar structure and sequence.

The covers and table of contents are the wrapping, similar to when one is given a gift and savors the giving before opening the package to reveal the contents.

Chapter 6

Presents from the Author

The drawing power of the first page or first few pages should convince the readers that the book is for them and that every moment spent reading will be worth the time and effort. Readers seldom give an author a second chance to reclaim their interest and commitment, so it is essential that readers immediately feel some confirmation of their predictions or expectations of the book and a trust that the author will not disappoint them.

The immediacy of involvement and commitment may come from the author making the readers feel as if they already know the characters, as in Charlotte Brontë's opening words of *Jane Eyre* (2003, originally published in 1847):

> *There was no possibility of taking a walk that day. We had been wandering, indeed, in the leafless shrubbery an hour in the morning; but since dinner (Mrs. Reed, when there was no company, dined early) the cold winter wind had brought with it clouds so somber, and a rain so penetrating, that further outdoor exercise was now out of the question.*

The readers here feel as if they are just reading another incident in a sequence of events in which they are already participants. This assumed familiarity with characters or previous incidents is sometimes conveyed by omitting any scene setting or introduction of characters. For example, in Figure 6.1, *Hoketichee and the Manatee* (Moeller 1998) begins with:

Hoketichee lowered herself into the river.

Hoketichee lowered herself into the river.

Figure 6.1: Pages 2 and 3 of *Hoketichee and the Manatee*

Dialogue is sometimes used as the initial hook to draw readers into the action, as on the first page of *Proud Garments* (Anderson 1996):

> *"There's a dead bird outside my bedroom window," said Bianca. "It's been there for some time . . ."*

But there needs to be a fine balance between the assumptions made and what the readers bring. For example, within the first page, Charlotte Brontë details the characters that comprise the "we" of the second sentence by drawing a clear picture of the relationships. The fine balance of assuming and explaining is critical in books used for the teaching of reading.

From those in the earliest stages of development to those most skilled, students must see themselves as the makers and interpreters of meaning. They should understand that teachers can show them how to access meaning and authors can include hooks within the text, but no one can make meaning for another reader.

Familiar introductory phrases often make readers feel as if they are co-authoring what is about to come. The words "once upon a time" immediately raise expectations of the problem-and-solution structure with contrasting characters of rich and poor, handsome and ugly, kind and cruel, weak and strong, or large and small. There is anticipation of more than one attempt to solve the problem, with magic being the turning point as the lesser character triumphs and "lives happily ever after." "Long ago in a far away land" signals fantasy and often a story with some similarity to the traditional fairy tale.

Authors sometimes try to gain immediacy by starting with the high point of an incident, returning later to provide background information. Other authors use scene-setting descriptions or character introductions to establish a knowing "nod-nod, wink-wink" between the pen and the reader. J. K. Rowling provides an example of this behind-the-scenes relationship between author and reader in *Harry Potter and the Philosopher's Stone* (1997):

> *Mr. and Mrs. Dursley, of number four, Privet Drive, were proud to say that they were perfectly normal, thank you very much. They were the last people you'd expect to be involved in anything strange or mysterious, because they just didn't hold with such nonsense.*

The authoritative tone set with the words "thank you very much" encourages readers to trust the author. This establishment of trust within the first few paragraphs or pages is as important in informational text as in fiction. A definitive statement can persuade the readers that the author has sufficient knowledge to make the text worth sharing (Opat 2000):

> *Minibeasts are tiny creatures that can be found almost anywhere—on land, in the ground, in the air and in the sea.*

Starting a text with a statement assumes the readers will trust the author. It is clear that the author has important information to share and will probably do so without condescending, as a series of introductory questions often appears to do, especially those beginning with "Did you know . . . " . The sentence "Minibeasts are . . ." has a clear link with the title, *Minibeasts,* and is likely to treat the readers and the content with respect.

Authors of informational text often use the initial pages to establish themselves as knowledgeable and credible, worthy of being "heard" as well as conveying some idea of how their information will be presented. The initial sentences of an informational text should give the readers a clear idea of the focus of the text and an indication of the writing style. The readers are then able to consider whether the text is likely to answer their questions or satisfy their interest. These initial sentences will help the readers decide if they will need to read carefully because of the density of the information or if it is likely to be a piece for skimming.

The pond is calm.   The pond is still.

2   3

Figure 6.2: Pages 2 and 3 of *The Pond*

A book for beginning readers should have the same immediate appeal as a bestseller for adults. The minimal text means few words can be devoted to scene-setting. At the same time, the first pages cannot carry all of the challenges, or students will consider the book too difficult and quickly lose interest and reduce effort. In cases where there are too many challenges on the first pages for a particular group of students, the teacher should "read the students into the text" by providing extra support and explanation. If sequence is not critical in an informational text, the pages can sometimes be read in an order more appropriate for the students. For example, the right-hand page of the first double opening of *The Pond* (Boland 1997) shown in Figure 6.2, "The pond is still" will be an easier entry point for many students than the left-hand page that reads "The pond is calm," because "still" is a more familiar word and it is easier to decode phonetically.

The first pages of longer texts, such as chapter books, with a number of characters should clearly describe relationships and provide sufficient identifiable markers for readers for reference if confusion occurs later. Some books include a genealogy chart or family tree or a map if frequent changes of scene are critical for comprehension.

Whatever the content, form, or writing style, authors need to convince their readers that a present awaits and that it is not only worth opening but also just right for that particular moment—a present for the present.

Chapter 7

Presents from the Illustrator and Designer

Illustrations and graphics are often the initial attraction to a book or text. Frequently they become essential elements when determining the suitability of a text for instructional purposes or when deciding how to present a text to a student or group of students. Initial considerations when selecting material for beginning readers may include the size of type, whether the typeface is serif or sans serif, spacing between words and lines and around illustrations, the degree to which the illustrations reflect or match the text, the number of visual features, the amount of text, and its placement in relation to the illustrations and the page.

> ***Visual language**—messages conveyed graphically (the primary function within the context of this book) or through moving and shaping (as in film and drama).*

It is generally accepted that illustrations in books for beginning readers should be placed above or before the relevant text and should not intrude on the text. The margins around the text should be wide enough for students to hold the book without covering the text. The text should not run close to the spine. This characteristic is especially so in thicker paperbacks that do not open flat. The page should not be crowded. A sentence carried overleaf (from one right-hand page to the next left-hand page) should not be able to be confused with the beginning of a new sentence on the right-hand page of the new opening. Text split above and below the illustration is considered to increase the level of challenge. The illustrations should match and clarify the text, as these often carry the main story line, with the text serving as captions or summaries of the action. But no matter how much information or story line the illustrations carry, it is important that they lead the readers to the text.

Authors for young readers rely on illustrators to help make the text more accessible to their audience. Many children love poring over detailed illustrations. However, the books used for the teaching of reading need to strike a balance between illustrations that convey too much information and those that are too minimalist or impressionist. The author's main message should receive prominence and

4

Figure 7.1: Page 4 of *Greedy Cat*

be presented with attention to cultural perspectives, balance of gender, and concern for safety and health issues.

A subplot included in the illustrations adds interest, often making a framework for students to write a complementary text, but the author's message should remain paramount. Sometimes the illustrative subplot introduces a new character, adding humor or acting as the catalyst for dialogue reflecting another level or dimension of comprehension. This is the case in *Greedy Cat* (Cowley 1983), as shown in Figure 7.1, when the young child (who does not feature in the text) is the only one who sees the cat eating the food from the mother's bag and is trying to attract the adults' attention. The inclusion of the child in these illustrations also brings an immediacy of "seeing oneself in the book" to the otherwise adult characters.

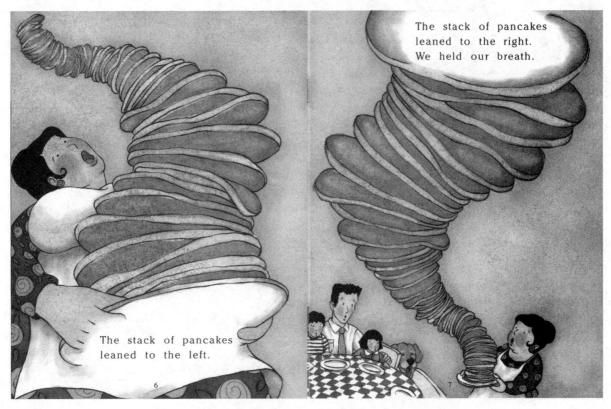

The stack of pancakes leaned to the right. We held our breath.

The stack of pancakes leaned to the left.

Figure 7.2: Pages 6 and 7 of *Pancakes for Breakfast*

The style of illustration should reflect or complement the mood and content of the text. The realistic and gentle illustrations in *The Birds at My Barn* (Moeller 2000) (shrink-wrapped with this publication) reflect the thoughtful nature of the text. On the other hand, the jovial and exaggerated content and style of Susan Kathleen Hartung's illustrations in *Pancakes for Breakfast* (Silvano 2000) extend the absurdity of the text. A pile of pancakes would completely collapse or slide off the plate before it "leaned to the left" or "leaned to the right," as shown in Figure 7.2.

They gnawed and cut down trees with their long, orange teeth. Then they used the logs and branches of the trees to build a dam across a stream and make a lake.

3

Figure 7.3: Page 3 from *A Family of Beavers*

Many books for young readers are being published with photographs rather than commissioned illustrations. The photographs do bring a real-life immediacy and credibility to the text, but the selection of books within the school setting should include some that include illustrations that students could use as models for the illustrations for their writing. Figure 7.3 shows how Gay W. Holland's illustrations in *A Family of Beavers* (Jackson 2002) mirror the specifics of the text while at the same time are clear enough for students to recreate in their own way.

The trio of author, illustrator, and reader is critical in any reading, but when the text and the illustrations are in harmony, there is more chance for the readers to be in harmony with the text and with the act of reading.

When selecting fiction text for skilled readers, teachers may consider the cover illustration, the density of the text on a page, and the placement of illustrations in relation to the matching text. However, the nature and amount of illustrative material and visual elements will probably feature more prominently when selecting informational text, especially if it is to be used in curriculum areas beyond reading or literature studies.

Text Forms and Features: A Resource for Intentional Teaching (Mooney 2001) describes the purposes of many text types and visual features. However, many books designed for middle-grade and upper-grade readers include several different illustrative features in a book and often on a page. When selecting material, teachers should consider the clarity of and access to each visual feature and the text. Unless the book is designed to be pictorial or the focus is intended to be the graphical features, the text should assume and retain priority, with the visual features clarifying, expanding, summarizing, or exemplifying the written information.

The copy of *Minibeasts* (Opat 2000) included with this book uses visual features that support the text in each of these ways. The diagram on page 13 of *Minibeasts* clarifies what an ant farm looks like when the directions in the text are followed. The labeled diagram on the previous page showing the cross-section of a beehive includes information extra to the text. "The News Cartoon" on page 4 summarizes information found elsewhere in the publication, while the two illustrations on page 11 exemplify the statement made in the text that butterflies and moths are "distant cousins." (Other features of *Minibeasts* are included in the descriptions of the book in Chapter 15: *Minibeasts*—A Magazine for Dipping and Delving . . .)

NEWS EXTRA

Raving about Rainforests **5**

Logging, slashing and burning

Why all the destruction?

THE GOVERNMENTS of many countries sometimes sell products taken from the rainforests. They do this to make money to help relieve the poverty of their people.

The rainforests are treated like a giant treasure chest that is raided over and over again —until no treasure is left.

Rainforests also contain many trees that are chopped down to make timber for firewood, furniture and housing. Much of it is also used to make wood chips and paper.

Timber from the rainforests is used by the local people and is also sold in large amounts to other countries. To get the timber, loggers often destroy everything in their path just to get one or two valuable **hardwood** trees. Bulldozers show no mercy as they move through and destroy the rainforest.

Another destructive practice is slash-and-burn farming. This is perhaps the biggest threat to the rainforest. It is a method of clearing the land that farmers use so they can have more farmland. They chop down the useful trees and plants and burn what is left.

They use the land to run huge herds of cattle and to grow crops. But rainforest soil is thin and loses its nutrients once the trees have gone. It is only useful to farmers for a few years before it is **infertile**.

The farm quickly becomes a wasteland, which cannot feed cattle or grow crops. This forces the farmers to look for more land. So they go deeper into the forest and start again.

Ahead of them, the rainforest shrinks. Behind them, the wasteland grows.

Fact of the day

In September 1987, a satellite picture of the Amazon Basin showed 7,603 fires burning in the rainforest.

Farmers often use fire to clear the rainforest to make room for crops and grazing land. As well as destroying the trees and plants of the rainforest, the fires threaten all the animals, birds and insects that live there.

Figure 7.4: Page 5 of "Logging, slashing and burning" in *Raving about Rainforests*

Some illustrative material matches the text not only in content but also in the skill required for comprehension. For example, the "compare and contrast" skill required for understanding the text of "Logging, slashing and burning" in *Raving about Rainforests* (Marcus 2002) is also necessary to comprehend the two-part photograph accompanying the text shown in Figure 7.4.

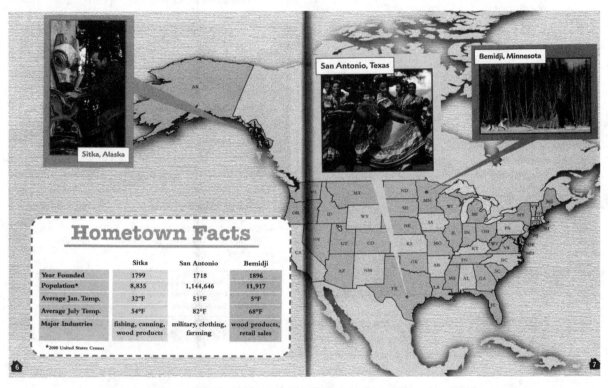

Figure 7.5: Pages 6 and 7 of *Hometowns*

Directionality is often thought to be a skill only for beginning readers, but some informational books and textbooks for fluent readers provide a challenge in what should be read first. The number of typefaces and visual features can crowd out the text and be confusing to both skilled and struggling readers. The use of color and type size of headings and subheadings, delineation of columns, and the placement of supplementary information can assist readers to break the information into manageable sections, understand the links

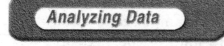

Analyzing Data

Life Spans of Human Cells

Like all organisms, cells have a given life span from birth to death. In multicellular organisms, such as humans, the health of the organism depends on cells not exceeding their life span. This is especially true of cells that tend to divide rapidly. If these cells did not die on schedule, overcrowding of cells would occur, causing uncontrolled growth that would be life-threatening.

The data table shows the life spans of various human cells. It also contains information about the ability of the cells to multiply through cell division.

1. **Inferring** White blood cells help protect the body from infection and disease-producing organisms. How might their function relate to their life span?

2. **Comparing and Contrasting** Based on the data, how are the consequences of injuries to the heart and spinal cord similar to each other? How are they different from the consequences of injuries to smooth muscle?

3. **Formulating Hypotheses** Propose a hypothesis to account for the data related to the cell life spans of the lining of the esophagus, small intestine, and large intestine.

Life Spans of Various Human Cells

Cell Type	Life Span	Cell Division
Lining of esophagus	2–3 days	Can divide
Lining of small intestine	1–2 days	Can divide
Lining of large intestine	6 days	Can divide
Red blood cells	Less than 120 days	Cannot divide
White blood cells	10 hours to decades	Cannot divide
Smooth muscle	Long-lived	Can divide
Cardiac (heart) muscle	Long-lived	Cannot divide
Skeletal muscle	Long-lived	Cannot divide
Neuron (nerve cell)	Long-lived	Most do not divide

4. **Going Further** Cancer is a disease related to cell life span and cell division. If cancer cells were added to the data table, predict what would be written under the columns headed "Life Span" and "Cell Division." Explain the reasoning underlying your predictions.

10–2 Section Assessment

1. 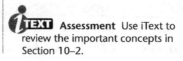 **Key Concept** Name the main events of the cell cycle.

2. **Key Concept** Describe what happens during each of the four phases of mitosis.

3. Describe what happens during interphase.

4. What are chromosomes made of?

5. How do prokaryotic cells divide?

6. **Critical Thinking Comparing and Contrasting** How is cytokinesis in plant cells similar to cytokinesis in animal cells? How is it different?

iTEXT **Assessment** Use iText to review the important concepts in Section 10–2.

Take It to the NET

Read about the relationship between the enzyme telomerase and the process of cell division. Then, construct a time line of the scientists who contributed to this discovery. Use the links provided in the Biology area at the Prentice Hall Web site for help in completing this activity: **www.phschool.com**

Figure 7.6: Page 247 from *Biology*, a high-school textbook

between the sections, and determine priority and sequence of reading. The selection of material for instruction and practice should include clear examples of each of these considerations. The double-page spread from *Hometowns* (Jackson 2002) shown in Figure 7.5 would be suitable for showing students how the three visual features are interdependent.

The page from *Biology* (Miller et al 2002) in Figure 7.6 provides an example of how the author and designer work together to remind readers of their role in accessing and considering the content. In the top section, the clarity of layout, the proximity of the data table to the associated tasks and questions, the introductory explanations of content and explanation of the table, and the thinking strategy

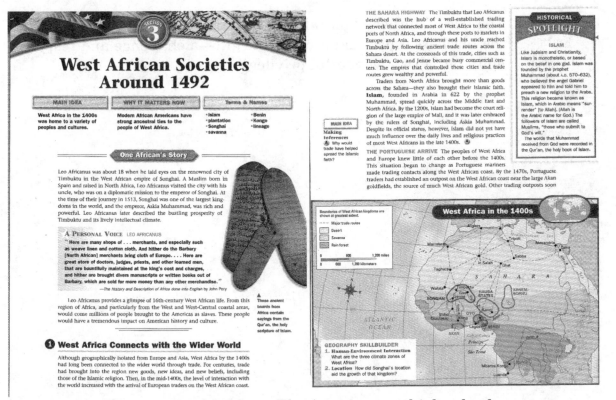

Figure 7.7: Pages 14 and 15 from *The Americans*, a high-school social studies textbook

prompts support the readers without minimizing the main learning focus on analyzing data. The lower section also maintains a focus on learning, informing the readers about what is being assessed and of relevant resources.

Although the layout of the pages in Figure 7.7 from a social studies textbook (Danzer et al 2003, 6-7) may appear more difficult, care has been taken to provide a focus for the reading, to lead the reader through the content, and to use different type faces and visual features to indicate a change of perspective, voice, or intention. The first two boxes, labeled "Main Idea" and "Why it Matters Now," remind readers of the "so what" implications of history, aiding the sorting and sifting of information to determine what needs to be remembered.

The trio of author, illustrator, and designer create the present and the teachers select and present the gift—a challenge and responsibility but also a wonderful privilege.

Chapter 8

The Present Itself

Authors use many different techniques to maintain their readers' commitment to the reading and to exploring the ideas and information presented. The conventions of the text type (expository, procedural, narrative, and so on) and its main shape (such as cumulative, sequential, or cyclic) provide an underlying rhythm and framework to carry the main message. But into that scaffolding, authors weave their own patterns and techniques, choice of vocabulary and language and sentence structures, and their unique "nod-nod, wink-wink," prompting their readers when thought beyond or behind the text will enhance understanding. These techniques give the piece "voice," whereby the author initiates a dialogue, stirring the readers to feel drawn to read and think actively, internalizing what they read as they sort and sift what the author is telling them and what they already know and think. It is through the voice of a piece that the author gains the reader's trust and empathy for the message.

Common techniques authors use to maintain their readers' commitment to continue the dialogue include repeating or changing the order of words, sounds, and structures. The most common umbrella distinction in educational books is between natural language and book language, as in the first two sentences of *Greedy Cat* (Cowley 1983).

Mum went shopping and got some sausages.
Along came Greedy Cat.

This juxtaposition of structure between the natural language in the first sentence and book language in the second creates a rhythm that, when repeated at the beginning of each of Greedy Cat's thieving escapades, gives beginning readers a signal that they are "with" the author, unfolding the plot as if it were their own. The ensuing familiarity with the structure soon has "Along came" being used as part of the readers' natural patterning in both spoken and written language. The inclusion of natural language and book language within a text helps learners extend the range of familiar structures and enables them to make an easy transition to poetry and to the language of literature. Familiarity with book language also helps students develop an individual voice in their writing. Most adults have phrases from books that roll off their tongues, or when hearing the first word of a favorite phrase or quote from a book, it brings an almost automatic recall of the rest of the phrase or quote.

While adding charm to a book, the exclusive or almost exclusive use of book language can increase the difficulty level on the first reading, but at the same time the delight of hearing and feeling such structures roll off the tongue can become the hook that draws readers back, as shown in Figure 8.1 from the book *Watermelon* (Cox 2000, 2-9).

> *Small are the seeds we plant in the ground.*
> *Green are the leaves on the vine.*
> *Yellow are the flowers that make the fruit.*
> *Striped are the melons that grow.*
> *White is the rind. It is thick and hard.*
> *Red is the sweet part we eat . . .*

The content of this piece allows for a clear and precise text/illustration match, reducing the difficulty and helping readers understand the sentence structure.

Book language provides an opportunity for teachers to ask students, "How else could the author have written this?" A teacher asked this question of a group of first-grade students. Their suggestions are

Small are the seeds
we plant in the ground.

Green are the leaves
on the vine.

Figure 8.1: Pages 2 and 3 from *Watermelon*

listed below. The teacher wrote each sentence on Post-it® notes, which were then attached to the appropriate page:

> *The leaves on the vine are green.*
> *The green leaves are on the vine.*
> *The vine has green leaves.*
> *Green leaves are on the vine.*
> *The vine's leaves are green.*

At the end of the lesson, the Post-it® notes such as those in the examples in Figure 8.2 were all placed on the inside cover for students to create their own supplementary story when revisiting the book. As the

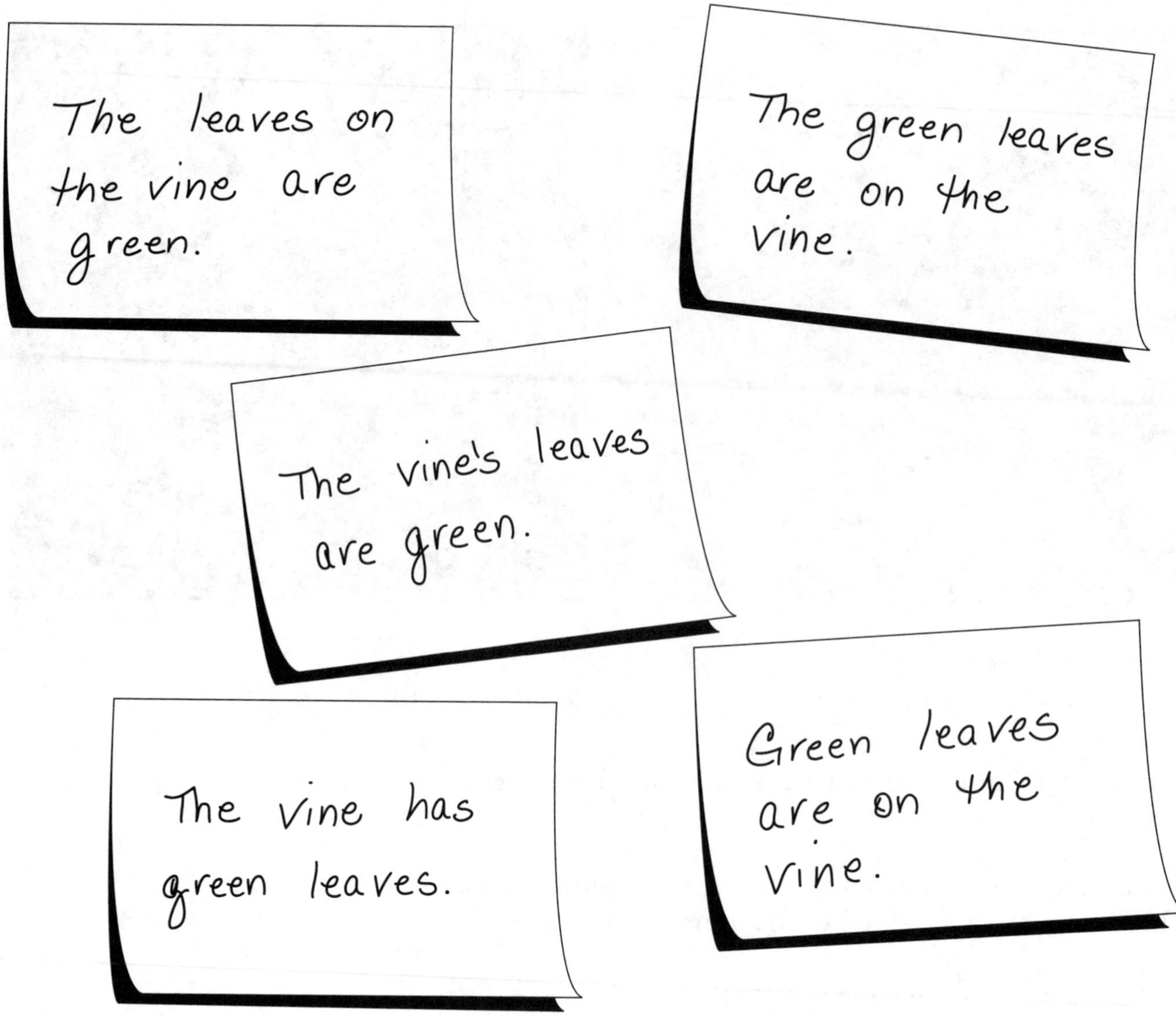

> The leaves on the vine are green.

> The green leaves are on the vine.

> The vine's leaves are green.

> The vine has green leaves.

> Green leaves are on the vine.

Figure 8.2: Students' suggestions for rewriting

teacher explained how they could use their sentences to create a second text through the book, one student said, "But we think 'green are the leaves on the vine' is dancing language and just right for this book."

Experiences such as these that the students enjoyed with *Watermelon* afford opportunities for readers to think and learn more about how language works rather than merely reading to get content. It moves gaining the author's message into an interactive dialogue, with the readers internalizing what is read, turning it to their own thinking and language patterns, and comparing these with those expressed in the text. Comprehension moves from "receiving meaning" to "knowing it as I see it," or what I call "understanding beyond knowing." The way the author crafts the language through the pen provides hooks similar to those on Velcro® tape, with one side of the tape remaining firmly attached. Readers are able to move away from a phrase or idea, consider it in the light of their understanding, and move back to the text without losing the thread. Figurative language is one of the most common hooks or techniques used in that crafting. When the author includes an example, it is often a signal for the reader to ask, "Do I see it like that?"

Figurative language *—structures or words that cause the reader to make comparisons, create images, or evoke expression or emphasis.*

Considering elements of figurative language in more detail alongside the knowledge of their students' language structures helps teachers confirm or amend the suggested level and approach of material. The number and frequency of familiar and unfamiliar elements contribute to the difficulty and manageability level of a text for a particular group or student at a particular time.

The simile is one of the most common figures of speech that authors use in fiction and informational material designed for the teaching of reading. At the early levels of development, students need to know that the words "like" and "as" may signal the author's intention to make a comparison. Later they can be helped to see that authors include similes to slow the reading. The inclusion of a simile causes readers to create a mental image of the two attributes or objects and consider whether they see it in the same way as the author. An author uses similes to control the readers in order to ensure the point is at least being considered thoughtfully or understood in more depth. It is impossible to read a simile quickly, even if both elements are familiar. And it is difficult to read a simile without changing one's intonation, as in C. S. Lewis' *The Lion, the Witch, and the Wardrobe* (1998, 116):

> *The shield was the colour of silver and across it there ramped a red lion as bright as a ripe strawberry at the moment when you pick it.*

A simile is an invitation for readers and author to consider simultaneously a perspective, but a metaphor is the author stating what the author perceives as a fact. There is not time for the readers to reflect. They may reread the phrase or section of text, but the author sees only one view to be necessary. The picture is painted and the ink dry (a metaphor in this context), and as is in this excerpt from *Harry Potter and the Philosopher's Stone* (Rowling 1997, 132):

> *They had reached the portrait of the Fat Lady.*
> *"Pig snout," they said and entered.*

Several figures of speech can be used to indicate the author's bias or where emphasis is required for full understanding. These may include an overstatement or exaggeration through a hyperbole. Hyperboles are frequently included in fantasy texts or in personal writing such as autobiographies, diaries, recounts of experiences, or in poetry.

> *"... if she knew about you four, your lives wouldn't be worth a shake of my whiskers!"* (Mr. Beaver talking to Peter) (Lewis 1998, 89)

Irony not only indicates emphasis but also is an author's ploy to heighten characteristics or implicitly indicate sarcasm.

> *"Just bring them along to the two hills—a clever boy like you will easily think of some excuse for doing that—"* (Lewis 1998, 47)

Such an insertion in a text causes readers to almost sneer as they read. Sometimes a carefully crafted situation, which turns out to be the opposite of what is usual or anticipated, creates its own irony. For example, many fables are based on irony. In the well-known fable "The Lion and the Mouse," it is ironic that the lion that had scared but spared the mouse had to eat humble pie when the mouse was the only one who came to rescue the lion. Many versions of this fable include statements of irony, such as:

> *"How could you, a little mouse, help me? Why I am the king of all the animals!"*

This fable also provides an example of the way authors use anthropomorphism to convey morals or abstract content. If the same concept were conveyed in a realistic incident, it could appear didactic or moralistic. Authors often use personification for the same reason.

Repetition is another technique authors use to gain the interest and support the staying power of their readers. Repetition of words, sounds, phrases, and sentences signals emphasis as well as aids memory, and sometimes this repetition creates an acquaintance or affinity with the author or a similar situation. The development of phonemic and phonological awareness, essential to decoding in reading and encoding in writing, is dependent on distinguishing repeated sounds within words.

The internal rhyme in the names Flopsy, Mopsy, and Cottontail in Beatrix Potter's *The Tail of Peter Rabbit* (originally published in 1902) means that, once familiar with the story, the mere sound of the word "Flopsy" makes the other two names come into one's thoughts, sometimes leading one to play with other possibilities, such as "Wopsy" or "Blopsy" and so on.

The rhythm of language created by the repetition of the word "berry" in Bruce Degen's *Jamberry* (1995) puts readers into a light-hearted mood for the happy-go-lucky berry picking expedition of a young boy and a bear:

One berry
Two berry
Pick me a blueberry
Hatberry
Shoeberry
In my canoeberry . . .

Repetition of sounds is the basis of assonance, internal rhyme, and alliteration in texts for more competent readers, as in Robert Frost's "Blue-Butterfly Day" (1969):

It is blue-butterfly day here in spring,
And with those snow-flakes down in flurry on flurry
There is more unmixed color on the wing
Than flowers will show for days unless they hurry.

But these are flowers that fly and all but sing:
And now from having ridden out desire
They lie closed over in the wind and cling
Where wheels have freshly sliced the April mire.

Or, from *Jane Eyre* (Brontë 2003, 206), originally published in 1847:

. . . and all of them had a sweeping amplitude of array that seemed to magnify their persons as a mist magnifies the moon.

These memorable moments of meaningful, skillfully crafted language become hooks as readers anticipate further examples of a wordsmith's craft.

Repetition of sentence structure is common in books for beginning readers. These books, often labeled as predictable, are designed to minimize challenges by limiting the change to the same word function or phrase from sentence to sentence and, usually, from page to page. Sometimes the story line is diluted to provide the consistent

Figure 8.3: Cover of *Pigs Peek*

framework, and sometimes the final pages include an increased number of challenges to provide a credible punch line. Either way, the books serve an important function in providing practice of basic vocabulary and sentence structure, as the changes are usually high-interest words or those that do not need to be mastered to the stage of automaticity at this level of the readers' development. *Watermelon* (Figure 8.1) is an example of a predictable structure, although many text patterns designed for very young readers have only one change in each sentence. Rhonda Cox's *Pigs Peek* (1996) is an example of a repeated structure with a one-word change on each page until the final two pages. She has also included repetition of the title, presumably for emphasis and to give the beginning reader a boost to the feeling of "I know this."

Pigs sleep.   Pigs peek.

6   7

Figure 8.4: *Pigs Peek,* pages 6 and 7.

Pigs sit.
Pigs stand.
Pigs peek.
Pigs dig.
Pigs sleep.
Pigs peek.
Pigs scratch.
Pigs peek.
Pigs do lots of things.
But mostly, these pigs peek.

Authors who write for older readers also use repetition. Sometimes it is used for emphasis, while at other times it is used to cause thought or create mood. Many couplets or stanzas of poems, passages of scripture, and verses of hymns are based on a repeated phrase, question, or sentence. For example, the final lines of the first three stanzas of Alfred, Lord Tennyson's "The Charge of the Light Brigade," written in 1864, are:

68

Into the valley of Death
Rode the six hundred.

The fourth stanza ends with repetition within the two lines and within a part of the previous three.

Then they rode back, but not—
Not the six hundred.

Sometimes rhyme is included, giving an extra opportunity for prediction and often allowing the repeated structure to be longer, as in the case of *Too Many Animals* (Lee 1999):

In come the animals
two by two—
one hippopotamus
and one kangaroo.
In come the animals
three by three—
two big cats
and a bumble bee . . .

Authors also help their readers maintain interest and effort by the way they break their work into sections, either through paging, punctuation (especially the ellipsis), paragraphing, chapters, parts within a book, scenes within a play, and the use of graphics and illustrative material (these two elements are discussed in Chapter 7 of this book)

Authors of books for early stages of reading development often include an ellipsis to introduce the climax or punch line of a text, indicating they want their readers to pause and think about the most likely conclusion to the episode. Authors of longer texts often signal their intention that readers should anticipate the unfolding of the next high point by replacing that ellipsis with a chapter ending. For example, in *The Lion, the Witch and the Wardrobe,* C. S. Lewis ends

Figure 8.5: Cover of *Too Many Animals*

the first chapter after describing the appearance of a key character and the opening words of dialogue between the new and familiar characters (1998, 18, 19):

> *One of his hands, as I have said, held an umbrella; in the other arm he carried several brown-paper parcels. What with the parcels and the snow it looked just as if he had been doing his Christmas shopping. He was a Faun. And when he saw Lucy he gave such a start of surprise that he dropped all of his parcels.*

"Goodness gracious me!" exclaimed the Faun.

Chapter Two

What Lucy Found There

"Good evening," said Lucy. But the Faun was so busy picking up its parcels that at first it did not reply.

Chapters or sections of informational text often end with a summary, allowing the authors to reiterate their main points and readers to revisit these facts before taking a breath and reading about another aspect of the topic.

Whether readers are supported through the text by transitions, repetition, or the crafting of language, authors have a responsibility in ensuring that once the book has been opened, their present can be enjoyed and savored. The gift of a text should not be a fleeting encounter but rather one that draws readers back again and again, drawing the same commitment from them as on the first reading.

Chapter 9

Presenting the Present

An important part of selecting material for classroom use is deciding the most appropriate approach to ensure that students assume as much responsibility as they are able to engage with the author's message.

APPROACHES

Independent approach—*opportunities to extend practice and exploration of skills and strategies acquired as a result of instruction in the more supportive approaches.*

Guided approach—*intentional individualized instruction within a small group promoting each student's continuous engagement with text and/or dialogue with the author and readers.*

Shared approach—*a detailed explanation by a more knowledgeable other of the thinking processes involved in accomplishing a task.*

Writing for—*a supportive approach, comparable to "reading to"; modeling a writer at work when a more skilled writer writes for one less able.*

Reading to—*a supportive approach where a skilled reader, acting on the author's behalf, reads to a less skilled audience. The ultimate goals are the enjoyment of the ideas and the way they are presented and motivation to savor the benefits of reading for oneself.*

Independent Approach

Reading material selected for any grade should include some that offers very few or no challenges, confirming students as successful readers and reminding them that reading is something they can do on their own whenever they choose to do so. Independent reading provides opportunities for students to initiate their own reading, and the material should allow students to pursue their individual interests as well as practice newly acquired skills and to read more about topics and themes currently being studied in the classroom. The material selected should include the writing forms and styles introduced during guided reading and the more supportive approaches of shared reading and reading to children. It should also include material that the students may have access to in their homes or in the community, such as brochures, magazines (sports, car, technology, handcraft, cooking), comics, timetables, and maps. It is important that students understand that the reading in the classroom is similar to that in life beyond the classroom and vice versa.

Most of the texts for independent reading should be easier than those for guided reading, although it is a good idea to include a few books at the students' instructional level so they can gain confidence in meeting unfamiliar text without extra guidance and support. It is suggested that the books for independent reading are stored separately from those for browsing, viewing, and reading in the classroom library where leveling of books does not assume such importance. Every time a book is selected from the independent book box, the student will be confirmed as a reader, knowing the text will be able to be read successfully. Every few weeks, the box could be emptied, with students discussing which were favorites and need to be kept in the box for further enjoyment, those that have not had initial appeal, which were difficult, and those that lead to further interest. This discussion would help the teacher select books to add to the collection and know which books might need some further "buy-in," through reading them to the students or discussing why they were selected. Sometimes the book selected simply does not hold sufficient appeal to attract the students. Knowing how to make a choice is an important part of developing critical readers and thinkers.

Guided Approach

The bulk of material selected for classroom use would be for the main instructional approach, often called guided reading. A greater number of supports than challenges means that the students are able to be the "code breakers" as well as the "meaning makers." However, these texts should be of increasing complexity, with challenges being introduced gradually but consistently. It is through this approach that students develop an expectation of the next challenge, a confidence in meeting that challenge, and a competence in doing so.

One of the key factors in my understanding of guided reading is that the material should offer the supports and challenges, and the teacher should offer only as much guidance as necessary for the students to be able to read hitherto unseen material successfully. This means that when selecting material for guided reading, teachers need to determine how the text supports the reader, the features that will probably offer some challenges, the nature and amount of prompting and explaining required to enable the reader to meet the challenges, and then how much practice the book provides to develop confidence and competence in applying the new learning.

For many teachers, this approach to selecting material requires a shift from giving priority to the level suggested by the publisher, choosing material because it fits in with a particular theme, that the book has worked well with other groups, that is has immediate appeal to the teacher, or that there is a "good" activity sheet readily available. When such criteria assume dominance, it means the students are not the focus of the instruction. In fact, they are expected to fit or be suitable for the material rather than the material be appropriate for the readers.

The material for guided reading should cover all curriculum areas in which the students will be required to gather information and complete related assignments. This support is especially important for students working with textbooks in which the number of textual and illustrative features can sometimes overwhelm readers. It may be that students are introduced to a chapter book or novel during a guided reading lesson and are assigned a chapter or section of the book to be read independently. (After all, sustaining effort over longer texts is one of the key skills and reasons for reading such material.) The next guided lesson focuses on introducing the next chapter in the science or mathematics textbook.

In guided or instructional reading, the relevance of content is important, but of equal if not greater priority is the acquisition of skills and strategies that enable students to access the content for themselves. The higher the grade level, the broader the range of content and forms in which the students are required to apply those skills independently and with automaticity and specific focus. This means material selected for all approaches at middle and upper grades needs to have strong links between the skills and strategies required to access the ideas and information across the different curriculum areas. For example, students learning about the functions in *Minibeasts*, as described in Chapter 15, need access to material that includes captions with similar functions in social studies. "Once is not enough" should be a mantra when selecting material for instructional purposes at any and every level.

Shared Approach

While guidance is the focus of the teacher's role in guided reading, support is the intent of shared reading when teachers explicitly explain how skilled readers meet and overcome challenges. The demonstrations and explanations should focus on the skills and strategies that the students will probably require to meet similar challenges in guided reading. For example, anticipating that the structure in *Watermelon* (Cox 1996)

> *Small are the seeds*
> *we plant in the ground*

would be a challenge for students when reading the book in guided reading, the teacher could select *Greedy Cat* (Cowley 1983) for shared reading to introduce the "book language" structure

Along came Greedy Cat.

As *Greedy Cat* is read and discussed, the teacher could explain how readers think of other ways that the author could say things and how this helps readers fully understand and appreciate the reasons for the text being as it is.

Aural language—*the receptive mode of oral language; vocabulary gained and understood through hearing it spoken or read.*

Critical to shared reading is a text with an identifiable structure and, in most cases, one offering as many challenges as supports. The supports in the text should be obvious enough to draw the students into the reading, allowing their energy to be expended on working through the new skill they are acquiring. And the teachers' explanations need to be matched to the students' developmental level, allowing them to be practiced in the collective readings. Limiting the selection of texts for shared reading to those that have a repeated pattern or are in the "predictable" category does an injustice to the intent of shared reading of broadening horizons, about the breadth and depth of reading, and of the benefits it accrues. Material selected for shared reading should instill a confidence that reading is worthwhile, that it is a here and now activity, and that books offer limitless wonders.

Reading to Students

The most supportive approach in the development and maintenance of readers is reading to students. The benefits of reading to students include the introduction of ways in which ideas, information, and experiences can be recorded through text and enjoyed through listening as a fluent reader recreates them. Students are able to enjoy and learn about their world and the worlds of others and of creatures and objects that they would not be able to access through their own reading. Material selected for this approach usually has more challenges for students than elements that would support their reading. However, the material should draw the students back to revisit it by themselves, offering delights through browsing, viewing, recreating the text as they are able, and discussing the text and/or illustrations with classmates. The material should be selected with as much care and forethought as that for any of the other approaches, because reading to students is comparable to the optimum advertisement for books as incomparable presents. When selecting material, teachers should be mindful of the students' interests, culture, and current experiences as well as items that will provoke discussion about what is happening around them. The continuing development of the students' oral and aural language is a key factor in the selection of material, and this is critical in terms of extending vocabulary as well as the myriad of ways authors use language to present ideas and information.

Classroom Text

Material selected for the classroom library and for general classroom use should also receive thoughtful consideration. Throughout any classroom day, students need access to material that provokes thought, offers comfort, confirms who they are and excites them about what they might become, values their culture, broadens their understandings and extends their knowledge, and enables them to pursue interests and complete assignments. These are all materials that can spur them to greater effort and independence. Thus, material within the classroom should include:

- Resources reflecting celebrations and customs of cultures represented in the school

- Dictionaries, including those in the languages the students speak and hear at home and at school
- Maps, including those of the local area
- Magazines, especially those matching students' interests
- Newspapers
- Encyclopedias of an appropriate difficulty level for browsing, researching, and detailed reading
- Books and visual and audiovisual resources on current and recent topics of study in all curriculum areas
- Students' writing including individual, group, and class efforts
- Teacher's writing that covers the forms students are expected to read and write
- Models of writing achievable by students
- Items of school interest and events
- Brochures, posters, timetables, and advertisement about the local environs and events.

It is not only what the material offers and the quality and relevance of content that is important. Of equal importance is the way in which they are displayed. Tatty material and tacky displays sell reading as a less-than-attractive option. If students are to see reading as a worthwhile pursuit, the material and reading itself must of the highest quality in every way, able to compete and stand out against other options. Students must see reading and books as presents they cannot resist.

Chapter 10

The Lasting Present

It is important that the criteria for selecting a book for use in an educational setting should include the range of continued thought and understanding that the material is likely to engender within the readers. This focus on ensuring meaningful thoughts about the author's message that linger within the reader differs from the traditional consideration given to the designated worksheet practicing a specific skill or the "neat" art activity that springs to mind when viewing the book. These may well have their place after the reading of a book. But most "real" readers do not rush to grab a pen to draw or complete a written exercise assigned by someone in a far-off office.

The consideration given to possible follow-up work should focus on how the topic, theme, issue, and style of the writing and/or illustrations might stir continued reflection and internalization within readers. The teachers' role is to anticipate how the author and readers might continue dialogue between and among themselves and then to plan options for how this continuing dialogue might be nurtured. As the teacher observes the readers' reactions to the reading and to what is read, some of the options might be eliminated and a clearer path surface, showing how to encourage and foster this continued thought or to help the readers consider what the book means and might continue to mean to them.

A book's residue will be as varied as the number of readers and, within any one reader, it will differ with each reading. Sometimes the residue will be the rekindling of a memory from a past experience sparked by a character trait or action. The original experience will be refreshed in the reader's mind and will continue to resurface from time to time. A character might even serve as a mirror of oneself or as a reminder of an acquaintance long since forgotten, but once remembered there is a desire to re-establish communication. At other times, a word, a phrase, or chunks of the author's language will resurface at the most unexpected moments, often engendering fleeting or more reflective thoughts about the content or style of the book or its underlying theme or issue.

Competent readers should have access to material that will elicit responses to:

- Author's craft—especially the techniques to attract the reader, maintain interest, control the reading, and support comprehension

- Reader's craft—what was learned about adjusting style and pace of reading to the content and/or writing style, the strategies that promoted successful reading, any new strategies used or practiced

- Illustrative material—in terms of content, style, and function

- Content—at several layers including topic, theme, and issue; characters, plot, setting, and mood; ideas, opinions, information, and events

- Format—design, layout.

Material for readers at earlier developmental stages should provoke reflection on the act of reading as well as on what has been read. Viewing material with these criteria in mind will keep teachers mindful of their role in developing avid and passionate readers rather than just lovers of books. The criteria will also assist teachers in moving beyond the thought, "this would be a good book for . . ." to, "what might this cause the students to think about, write about, talk about, and want to read . . . ?"

> **Developmental stages**—*indicators of a common pattern of acquisition though learning styles, experiences, and instruction that influence the pace and rhythm of progress.*

The frameworks shown in Figures 10.1 and 10.2 are examples of wall charts intended to help students consider their responsibility to think beyond the superficial. Teachers might also find them useful when selecting material that will cause students to respond in some depth. Once the students have had to assimilate the content and the way it was presented and to formulate some of their thoughts and new information, they could use the framework to de-

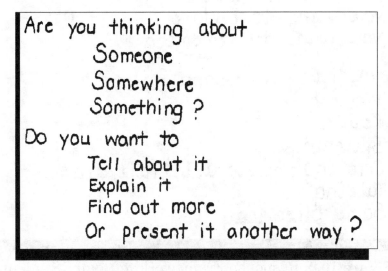

Figure 10.1: Response Framework for Younger Students

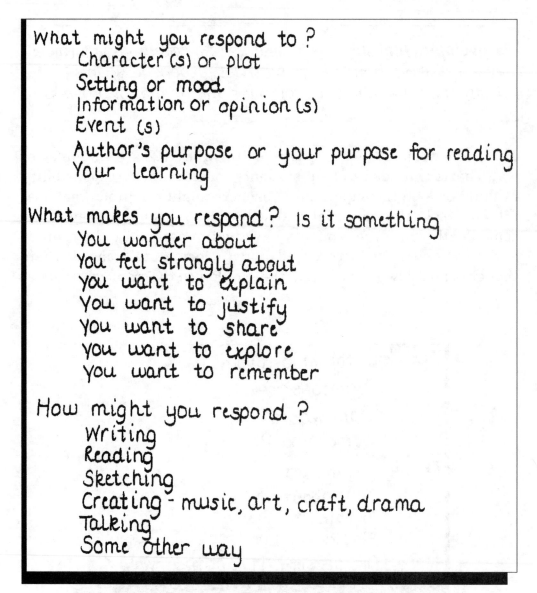

What might you respond to ?
    Character (s) or plot
    Setting or mood
    Information or opinion (s)
    Event (s)
    Author's purpose or your purpose for reading
    Your learning

What makes you respond? Is it something
    You wonder about
    You feel strongly about
    You want to explain
    You want to justify
    You want to share
    You want to explore
    You want to remember

How might you respond ?
    Writing
    Reading
    Sketching
    Creating - music, art, craft, drama
    Talking
    Some other way

Figure 10.2: Response Framework for Older Students

cide how to respond to a text. However, it should be understood that sometimes, after consideration, it could be that no response is necessary or that it is too premature. When using the framework, the students select one focus from each of the two sections to plan an oral, written, visual, or dramatic response. In the upper grades, once familiar with initiating a response, two items could be selected. Figure 10.3 shows how a fifth-grade teacher used the framework to help her students learn more about similes and initiate some of their own practice.

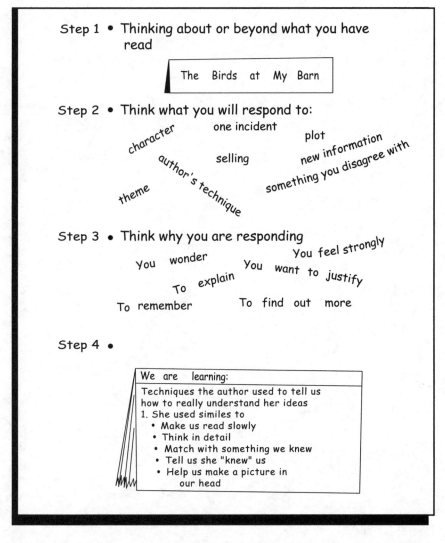

Figure 10.3: Using the framework to focus on one teaching point.

A book will only be a suitable present when it leaves a residue of thought and takes readers beyond what it says. Teachers need to ensure that students have sufficient opportunities to take the wrapping off the author's message and explore it for themselves.

Part II: *Using the Present*

Chapter 11

Choosing the Present

The title of this chapter may seem out of place. After all, one usually chooses a present before giving it, opening it, or enjoying it. However, it is only when one knows what a book really offers, the parts of it and the whole, that its true potential for helping readers gain competence and independence can be fully appreciated.

The last section of this book provides examples of thinking about some books in their entirety, focusing on what teachers might notice as they carefully view a book for possible use in a class setting. It is acknowledged that each pair of eyes will see different features, and teachers' knowledge of the students for whom material is being sought will scan for different aspects. However, the following "walk throughs" are offered as reminders of how much often goes unnoticed and how much we assume students will glean and understand but in reality require explicit intentional instruction. Each book or item is considered in a different way. As Part I of this book has shown, there is no formula for determining the level or suitability of material. The authors' hooks are different for each piece of writing. Those hooks shape how we view the writing as much as they influence the way a student interacts with the book. The examples have not tried to cover all aspects of reading, as that would be second-guessing what the students bring, especially in terms of decoding. The focus of the comments and suggested questions is on what the author and illustrator offer and on ways the teacher can prompt engagement at a suitable depth.

The first example, in Chapter 12, *The Hungry Sea Star* (Shahan 1997), highlights how an author and illustrator invite readers to think beyond the obvious and how teachers can use this to cause inferential thought within the readers. The letter format of the traditional tale of Red Riding Hood in Chapter 13 requires more sophisticated inferential reading and provides opportunity for readers to consider textual and illustrative detail. They can also focus on the role that background knowledge plays in helping access meaning. Chapter 14 provokes thought and discussion about the interdependent roles of reading and writing as well as providing suggestions to help readers understand the features of the autobiographical form. This informational piece is followed by notes in Chapter 15 about the magazine format of the *Minibeasts* edition of **The News** (Opat 2000). Features of text and illustration are the focus of the suggestions for this title. Chapter 16 shows there is a wealth of free material available that offers information of local and topical interest and relevance. The notes based on one publisher's catalogue will remind teachers of some of the learning opportunities that the free materials offer. The final example in Chapter 17 is a more detailed consideration of the features in *The Birds at My Barn* (Moeller 2000). The notes include suggestions for its use. Copies of *The Birds at My Barn* and *Minibeasts* are shrink-wrapped with this publication.

When reading the examples, it is important to remember that the questions and instructional notes will need to be amended for each and every group of students. It is the notes that can be manipulated, but never the student. There can be no kidding! It is the teachers' responsibility and privilege to make sure that students experience books as presents that can be opened time and time again, with each revisiting offering new insights into the pleasures of reading and of being a reader.

Chapter 12

The Hungry Sea Star—Encouraging Inferential Reading of Text and Illustration

Authors of informational text, and authors of fiction, trust their readers to read beyond the words and to make inferences from the text and illustrations. At first glance, *The Hungry Sea Star* (Shahan 1997) appears easier to read than the "Fluent 1" level suggested on the back of the book for the guided approach. However, a "walk through" of this short informational book reminds readers that the level is established by what the book does not say or illustrations do not show as much as by what is laid out.

Figure 12.1: Cover of *The Hungry Sea Star*

The Cover—Figure 12.1

Look carefully at the title and the illustration on the front cover. What do they lead you to expect about the kind of book this might be? What clues does the title of this book give you about the information you might gather?

The word "hungry" indicates the focus, and the definite article suggests it will be specific and about one sea star rather than being a general text about sea stars.

It is easy to see why this creature is called a sea star. I wonder if it has any other names. If you do not know of one, perhaps you could invent one. (The inside back cover shown in Figure 12.2 provides relevant information.)

What is unusual about a sea star?

Nonfiction Note
Sea stars used to be called *starfish*. But fish have gills and fins and scales and sea stars do not. So now they are called *sea stars*. A sea star may take hours to finish eating one mussel with its belly.

photo by Sherry Shahan

Figure 12.2: Inside back cover of *The Hungry Sea Star*

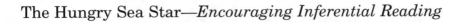

The Hungry Sea Star

by Sherry Shahan

illustrations by Gary Torrisi

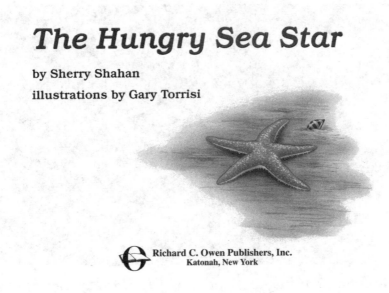

Richard C. Owen Publishers, Inc.
Katonah, New York

Figure 12.3: Title page of *The Hungry Sea Star*

The Title Page

Before you turn to the title page (Figure 12.3), *think about the setting shown on the cover. Now look at the illustration on the title page. What do those two pictures tell you?*

Pages 2 and 3

Even at this early stage, readers should be shown how informational text does not necessarily need to be read or discussed in sequence. This double opening shown in Figure 12.4 provides opportunity for starting with what is probably the easiest and more obvious text on page 3, and then returning to page 2.

Read these two pages to find out how the sea star was feeling.

Can you suggest another word the author might have used instead of "moved"?

A sea star moved across the ocean floor.

It was hungry.

Figure 12.4: Pages 2 and 3 of *The Hungry Sea Star*

Pages 4 and 5

Just as the text is more complex than it may first appear, so are the illustrations. On pages 4 and 5 in Figure 12.5, the mussel that the sea star has chosen to eat was seen on page 3. The rocks and sea plants are the same on both double openings.

What do you think the illustrator hoped you might have noticed in the illustrations on these pages and those on the previous ones? What thinking did you need to do beyond the words? What did the author think you already knew about mussels?

Pages 6 and 7

For some students, the split text and the word "oozed" may be the challenges on page 6 in Figure 12.6.

Figure 12.5: Pages 4 and 5 of *The Hungry Sea Star*

What do you notice about the way you will need to read this page?

Look at the illustration. What do you expect this page to describe?

Figure 12.6: Pages 6 and 7 of *The Hungry Sea Star*

Now read to discover what details the author has told you.

Which two words are action words (verbs)?

How did you work out the action word (verb) in the second sentence?

Can you think of another word the author could have used?

What has the author left for you to think about?

The sea star slowly slurped up all the soft and slimy parts . . .

and left two empty shells.

s l u r p

Figure 12.7: Pages 8 and 9 of *The Hungry Sea Star*

Pages 8 and 9

The alliteration of "slowly," "slurped," and "slimy" and the large type of "slurp" in the illustrations shown in Figure 12.7 would probably evoke discussion.

I wonder why the author put the words "slowly" and "slurped" together . . . And there is another word beginning with the same blend.

What did the author want you to do as you read that sentence?
What have these two pages told you about what the sea star eats?

The sea star moved across the ocean floor.

Figure 12.8: Pages 10 and 11 of *The Hungry Sea Star*

Pages 10 and 11

Think about what the author and the illustrator have told you about the way a sea star moves. What word could you use on this page instead of "moved"? (Figure 12.8)

Page 12

Students may need their attention drawn to the cyclic structure of the text, because the page break makes the repetition less obvious (see Figure 12.9).

It was hungry.

Figure 12.9: Page 12 of *The Hungry Sea Star*

Do you notice anything about the way the author ends this story?

Reread the last two sentences. Scan back through the book and see if you have read these anywhere else. Why did the author make this a text that ends where it began?

Postreading discussion could include how much extra information the illustrations conveyed and how much thinking the author left the readers to bring or infer. The idea of the text as a summary or set of captions could be discussed. The cyclic nature of the text and other cyclic texts would also engender meaningful discussion and application.

Chapter 13

"Dear Red Riding Hood"—There Is More to a Good Text Than the First Reading

Some texts are more suitable for asking a particular kind of question, thus focusing the student's attention on a particular strategy or kind of processing or comprehension. However, other texts provide opportunity for covering the gambit of literal, inferential, and analytical questions about decoding strategies, conventions of print and layout, understanding of content and genre, and illustrative material as well as questions from an author's perspective and those from a reader's point of view. In order to cover this range of questions in a lesson with sufficient time for discussion, the text usually needs to be shorter and at an easier level than text where the challenges are mainly in decoding.

Literal comprehension—as the author stated it, and as it can be cited in the text.
Inferential comprehension—the reader brings knowledge and understandings to add to or take from the text ideas and information not explicitly stated.
Analytical comprehension—a detailed consideration and evaluation of the ideas and information stated in text and of their presentation.

At first glance, "Dear Red Riding Hood" (McPherson 1998) appears to be a very easy text, and prior knowledge of the fairy tale would certainly help a reader cope with the unusual format of the piece. However, comprehension to the point of "understanding beyond knowing" lifts the text to another level of complexity. As I read the piece, thinking about what the author assumes the reader can add or fill in and the dialogue between author and reader about the way the text is constructed, I formulated some questions (*in italics)* and possible responses or transitions to keep the conversation going between teacher, acting on the author's behalf, and reader. I also noted (**in bold type**)

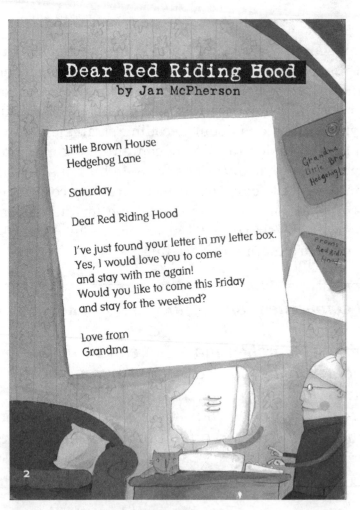

Figure 13.1: Page 2 of "Dear Red Riding Hood"

features that could form possible discussion points, now or later, in the reading. The comments in parentheses indicate whether the question requires literal, inferential, or analytical thought.

Page 2—Figure 13.1

How do we know this is not the first letter in this correspondence? Can you find two clues? (Literal). Grandma talks about the letter she found in her mailbox. The word "yes" is in response to something in a previous letter.

Figure 13.2: Page 3 of "Dear Red Riding Hood"

Page 3—Figure 13.2

Notice who wrote this second letter. What does that tell you about the letter in the red envelope? In your head, write the letter that you think might have been in the envelope. (Inferential)

The author assumes the reader can fill the gap, for example, that Red Riding Hood replied that she would like to come and may have asked what she could bring.

Note the layout of the list, introduced by the colon and with incomplete sentences contrasting with the list on page 5, where the complete sentences for the "rules" reflect the urgency of the content. This could be an introduction to, or reminder of, two of the several purposes and features of lists.

Page 4—Figure 13.3

Why is there no letter from Red Riding Hood this time? (Inferential)

There is no time for a response between the one on page 3 and the one on page 4.

And why is Grandma writing this letter by hand? (Literal)

What do you notice about the way the author describes how Grandma is feeling? (Analytical)

Use of alliteration

I wonder why the author described Grandma as having "sniffs and snuffles." (Analytical)

For emphasis

Figure 13.3: Page 4 of "Dear Red Riding Hood"

Page 5—Figure 13.4

When did Grandma write this letter? Find two clues. (Literal—text and illustration) Thursday in text and the moon in the illustration.

Use of dash for emphasis

What four signals does the author use on this page to let you know what she thinks are important parts? (Literal and analytical)

Exclamation mark, dashes, capital letters, and list of rules.

How do you know that Grandma is feeling better? (Inferential)

The text says she went out to her letter box that morning.

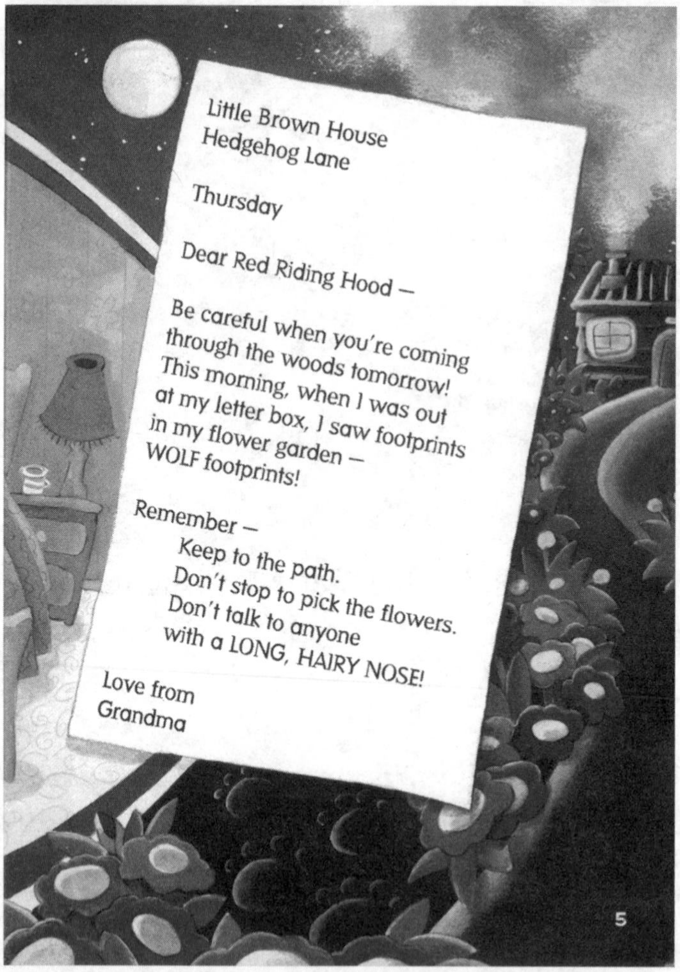

Figure 13.4: Page 5 of "Dear Red Riding Hood"

Figure 13.5: Page 6 of "Dear Red Riding Hood"

Page 6—Figure 13.5

How does Red Riding Hood know not to say anything to Grandma?
(Inferential)

Note Grandma in the illustration

What does the expression on Red Riding Hood's face suggest?
(Inferential)

I wonder if the wolf is awake or asleep. What do you think? Give reasons for your response. (Inferential and analytical)

Figure 13.6: Page 7 of "Dear Red Riding Hood"

Page 7—Figure 13.6

Note change in perspective

What do you think happened between pages 6 and 7? (Inferential)

How does this page differ from the usual story about Red Riding Hood? (Analytical)

There is one more letter on the next page. Who will write it and to whom will it be written? (Inferential and analytical)

Little Brown House
Hedgehog Lane

Saturday

Dear Mr Woodcutter

My friend, how can we ever thank you?

You arrived at my house yesterday
just in time to save my life.
Now the woods are free
of that cunning wolf at last!

My brave Red Riding Hood and I are going
to have a party this afternoon.
We want everyone in Hedgehog Lane
to come — especially you,
dear Mr Woodcutter.

Your grateful friends
Grandma and Red Riding Hood ✿

illustrations by Ali Teo

Figure 13.7: Page 8 of "Dear Red Riding Hood"

Page 8—Figure 13.7

Who do you think really wrote the letter? Justify your choice with two reasons. (Literal and analytical)

Grandma on behalf of herself and Red Riding Hood. She says "My brave Red Riding Hood and I . . . " and "You arrived at my house . . . "

Some readers may wonder about the need for such detail when reviewing a book. Every one of the comments or questions listed in this chapter is pertinent to a full understanding of this rendering of the traditional story. Noticing such detail in text and illustration is the level of understanding expected of students in much of their reading and writing. Looking at a piece of a book in this depth helps us anticipate features or elements that may provide a challenge and those that will probably give support, enabling the reader to engage in meaningful dialogue with the author.

Chapter 14

A Storyteller's Story—An Author's Autobiography for Budding Readers and Writers

Figure 14.1: Cover of *A Storyteller's Story*

The cover illustration and the title of *A Storyteller's Story* (Martin 1992) hint at the biographical form (and are confirmed in the **Meet the Author** logo), but the autobiographical feature is not evident until the first page of text. The title indicates a narrative, but the first page reveals it to be a narrative told in letter form. The road sign of the mammoth on the cover provides another touch of incongruity. (Does the author like mammoths? How could a contemporary road sign show an extinct animal? Does the author write about mammoths?) These three elements pique the readers' interest and are a reminder that a storyteller's story will surely provide some surprises. There is a touch of reality in the photograph, causing anticipation that there really will be a storyteller. The illustration on the title page shows the author with a supposedly life-sized mammoth in a museum, causing even more intrigue about the sign on the cover.

To tomorrow's authors
and storytellers

Figure 14.2: Page 3 of *A Storyteller's Story*

The dedication, "To tomorrow's authors and storytellers," personalizes the book for the readers, but is he referring to the dog as an author or storyteller? One cannot help but like this author, because he obviously has a sense of humor. And, on reflection, it becomes clear that he hopes his readers will become authors. Readers now know he likes mammoths, kayaking (from the back cover), and dogs.

Figure 14.3: Photo from back cover of *A Storyteller's Story*

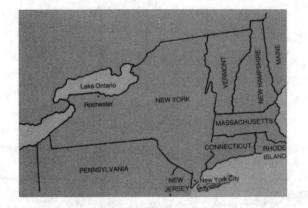

Dear Friends,
I'm an author and a storyteller.
Like you, I became a storyteller
as soon as I could talk,
and an author when I first wrote stories
in school.
My home is in Rochester, New York,
a city on the shores of Lake Ontario,
one of the Great Lakes
between the United States and Canada.

5

Figure 14.4: Page 5 of *A Storyteller's Story*

Pages 5 to 7

The phrase "Dear Friends" presents the letter format, and the first sentence moves the prediction of a biography to an autobiography. The remainder of the three pages provides information common to the introductory section of an autobiography—what he does, where he lives, and some personal information. Readers learn about his family, which conveys a "real person" message. These first three pages have features common to the beginning of a narrative—introductions of characters, scene setting, and mood.

Pages 8 and 9

These pages will probably elicit a great deal of discussion, with many students recognizing Rafe Martin's writing process as similar to their own. The "real-person" perspective established in the first few pages will be confirmed.

Sometimes a story almost seems to write itself.
Then my fingers can hardly keep up
with the flow of words in my mind.
It's very exciting to feel this happen.
Some mornings I spend my time
editing the stories I've already begun.
I walk around the room reading them out loud,
listening to the way they sound.

In the morning Rose and Ariya go off to school
and my writing day begins.
When I work on a new idea
I first picture the story in my mind,
then I write it.
Then I rewrite, carefully choosing words
that will help my readers
and my illustrator see the characters
and the story for themselves.
I rewrite a story many times,
to get it just right.

8

9

Figure 14.5: Pages 8 and 9 of *A Storyteller's Story*

Pages 10 to 32

The remainder of the book alternates between Rafe's life as an author and his life beyond or through writing. It highlights how an author is never totally divorced from his work, with ideas for writing coming at unexpected moments and from the ordinary events of life. The latter part of the text reminds the readers that writing is not always easy and is something to be worked at.

A Storyteller's Story provides readers with insights into an author's life through autobiographical writing. The following could be the focus of discussion with students:

- Autobiographies can focus on selected aspects of a person's life—they do not need to be presented as chronological life stories or cover everything about a person's work or life.

- Autobiographies allow authors to share what they perceive to be important about their lives and/or their achievements.

- Autobiographies can be told in a narrative form or, as in this case, as a narrative letter.

- Autobiographies usually focus on positive aspects of one's life.

- It is the details rather than the big picture that attract readers to an autobiography.

- A writer has total freedom about what they write about themselves in an autobiography.

- An autobiography usually focuses on what the person thinks and does rather than what other people think of him or her.

Chapter 15

Minibeasts—A Magazine for Dipping and Delving and for Detail and Comparison

The cover of **The News** edition entitled *Minibeasts* (Opat 2000), a copy of which is shrink-wrapped with this book, provides several clues about the content and the focus and style of the writing. The wording also hints that the author intends to use some literary devices to present an informational text. "Snail trails to slime time," "Lawless ladybirds," "To bee or not to bee?," and the suggestion that "cockroaches party all night" are not the usual introduction to the contents of a science book. The cover also indicates the format of the book. Pages 4, 6, 8, and 12 signal a collection of short pieces. The table of contents in Figure 15.1 entitled "Inside" confirms this.

This publication offers a range of text forms and features including:

- Table of contents
- Index
- Two forms of glossary—the conventional type of pronunciation guide and definition at the end of the book and the "Word of the day" on pages 2 and 10
- Advertisements—a birth and two wanted notices (see pages 5, 10, and 11)

Minibeasts EDITION

Debbie Opat

A word from our editor

MINIBEASTS are tiny creatures that can be found almost everywhere—on land, in the ground, in the air and in the sea.

Minibeasts are creatures that do not have backbones. Some have hard shells, and others are soft, like slugs. There are over a million different types living on our Earth.

Have you ever wondered how minibeasts can survive among people and animals that tower over them? Find out about these tiny creatures in this edition of *The News*.

Daily spot

Minibeasts inspire musicians! Adam Ant was a famous singer. Other bands are Iron Butterfly, The Beatles, Insect Surfers, Halo of Flies and Sting. Isn't that a buzz?

Figure 15.1: Table of contents from *Minibeasts*

- Facts about minibeasts presented as "Daily spot" (pages 1, 6, 7), "Fact of the day" (pages 9, 11, 12, shown in Figure 15.2), and "Did you know? (pages 9, 15, 16, 18)

- Further references—"Further resources" (page 22) reviews multimedia resources

- Editorial notes—"A word from our editor" (page 1) setting the focus of the magazine and an editorial (page 20)

- Letters to the Editor—page 20 and letters to the bug expert and his reply (page 21)

- Cartoons—"The News Cartoon" on page 4 is a summary of information presented in items throughout the book while the cartoon on page 19, "Dan Daily and his dog Scoop," is a short comic strip and a pun.

- Articles—some as expository texts; "Snail trails to slime time" on page 8 and others in a more lighthearted magazine style requiring inferential reading as in "Fashion Flash" on page 5. These form the bulk of the book.

- Procedural text—"Make your own ant farm" (page 13)

- Poem—"Minibeast trivia" (page 19)

- Jokes—(page 24).

Illustrations, diagrams, and photographs throughout the book clarify, extend, summarize, and exemplify the text. Ways in which captions in *Minibeasts* serve these functions were discussed in Chapter 7: Presents from the Illustrator and Designer.

Minibeasts offers opportunities for readers and writers to:

- Understand the function and nature of a magazine

- Compare the same information presented in different forms—"Level-headed ladybirds avoid enemies" and "Fashion flash"

- Infer factual information presented in fictional text—as in the advertisements of "Fashion flash"

To bee
or not to bee?

Who wants to live in a hive?

THOUSANDS OF honey bees live together in hives. These hives are like busy towns. The queen bee is in charge!

The queen bee mates with male bees called **drones**. A queen bee lives for about five years. She lays thousands of eggs during that time.

The other bees are worker bees. Worker bees feed the queen bee and look after her by licking her to keep her clean. They also take care of the young bees and fix, clean and guard the hive against wasps and other enemies.

Only females have a sting. Bees use their sting to protect their community.

Bees have barbs on their sting so it gets stuck in the skin of their enemies. Bees die after using and losing their sting.

Fact of the day

Bees talk by dancing. If they dance in a circle, it means food is nearby. Lots of tail wagging means food is far away.

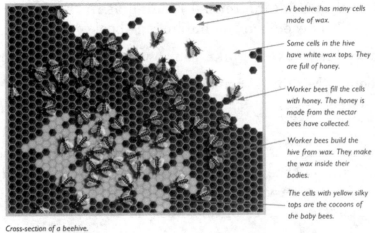

A beehive has many cells made of wax.

Some cells in the hive have white wax tops. They are full of honey.

Worker bees fill the cells with honey. The honey is made from the nectar bees have collected.

Worker bees build the hive from wax. They make the wax inside their bodies.

The cells with yellow silky tops are the cocoons of the baby bees.

Cross-section of a beehive.

Figure 15.2: Page 12 from *Minibeasts*

- Understand different ways of presenting summaries—cartoons, captions, labeled diagrams, advertisements

- Discuss the role of literary devices usually associated with fiction in informational writing

- Follow a procedural text and select a writing or illustrative form other than that usually used for recording the results

- Identify connections between texts—information, writing style, text focus, e.g., humor

- Discuss headings and subheadings

- Identify persuasive language and bias within informational texts

- Discuss the editor's role

- Write letters to the editor to be answered by classmates acting as editor or content experts

- Discuss how the role of the table of contents differs in an informational text from that in a novel

- Understand the function of columns and how these affect layout

- Consider page layouts and how this applies to their work

- Use the items as models for their own writing and illustrative work

- Design and create a magazine as a group project

- Reformat an informational text—add heading or subheadings, graphics, columns

- Discuss the back cover as a form of blurb

- Collect magazines and identify common elements

- Discuss subscriptions

- Differentiate between a magazine and a newspaper, between a textbook and a topical book.

As with any present, an element of surprise and challenge should remain for the next unwrapping. *Minibeasts* would be a great book for dipping and delving, for sharing with others, for browsing, for detailed reading, and for the sheer enjoyment of reading and talking with those who created the present.

Chapter 16

Free Gifts—There Is a Wealth of Reading in the Wider World

Although much of this book has focused on material in book form, there is a wealth of free material suitable for inclusion in resources for the teaching of reading. Not only does much of this free material offer short accessible examples of text features often included in text books or features we assume students can use in their everyday life but also much of the content has a special relevance for students.

Brochures, posters, sports pages from magazines and newspapers, travel timetables, catalogs, and newspaper advertisements provide material of interest to students of all ages and especially to students who are unable to maintain interest and effort on longer texts, or those who find little relevance in some of the fiction material used for instructional purposes. It is not suggested that advertising material should form the diet of a reading program, but selected items can supplement and complement the staple diet and provide hooks for some students.

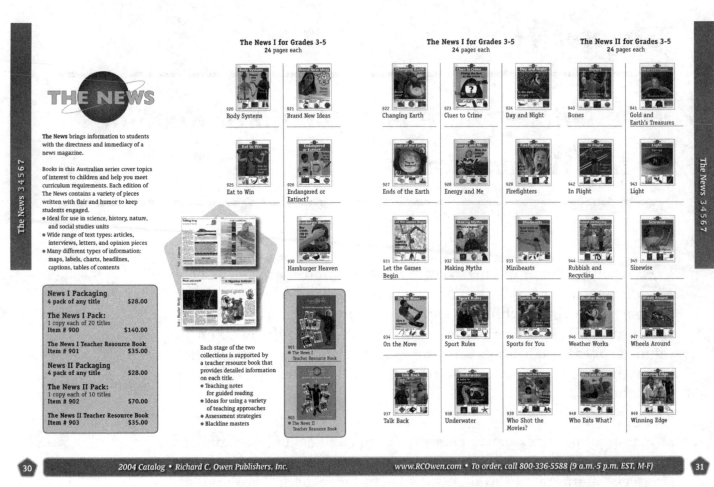

Figure 16.1: Pages from a book publisher's catalog

Involving students in the selection of new material to be purchased can introduce them to features of a catalog and help them understand some elements and purposes of persuasive language. The pages from a publisher's catalog shown in Figure 16.1 would be suitable for such a lesson with students in middle and upper grades.

These pages include the following features:

- Bullets listing characteristics of the product
- Abbreviations and codes—hash mark, Inc., EST, M–F, AM and PM, www
- Codes—grade references, item numbers
- Persuasive language used to market a product
- Persuasion through overt and implied language and assumptions
- Facsimiles to attract attention, remind readers of what may already be familiar.

The following lesson, led by a teacher, focuses on the elements of a catalog:

We have approximately three hundred dollars to spend on informational resources for our classroom. I thought we could consider this material displayed in this publisher's catalog. What connections did the word "catalog" trigger for you?

What might have been a more appropriate word than "displayed"?

What do we know about the kind of language commonly used in advertising?

Scan the text to find one example of persuasive language.

How does that influence the way you might read this page?

Scan the page again and find two more features that would not be common in a piece of fiction...in a book report.

When you first looked at these pages, what attracted your attention?

What made that part eye catching?

Which parts are you going to read closely given that we are thinking about buying more resources?

Before you make a decision about the title you might choose, what other parts of the page are important for you to access? What other information will help you know that you are making a good choice?

If you are buying more than one title, what options do you have?

Do you see titles that might have connections?

What did you need to know about features of text to get all of the information from this page?

Which parts of the pages are factual? How did you decide that?

Which information was essential and which was purely persuasive?

Make a list of the persuasive words or phrases. Then mark those that are very obviously intended to be persuasive, and use another mark to indicate those that are more subtle in their attempt to encourage you to buy.

What part did the book titles play in helping you select books?

Did you calculate that one package was more economical than another?

Chapter 17

The Birds at My Barn—*Putting It All Together*

Although the suggested level on the back cover of *The Birds at My Barn* (Moeller 2000), a copy of which has been shrink-wrapped with this publication, is listed as suitable for using at the fluent level, it is also appropriate for in-depth work in higher grades. The author uses a number of techniques to control the reading pace, signaling readers when to pause and ponder, to make comparisons, to make inferences, to consider illustrations, and to consider details. The book provides a clear model for older students writing a reflective and sequential observation in a personal and gentle voice.

This chapter describes how a teacher might view what a book offers, followed by a brief description of a group of sixth-grade students and what led the teacher to select the book. The third section lists some of the questions the teacher asked to provoke thought and discussion and some of the students' responses and contributions. This first lesson focuses on the reading/writing connection—what we learn from an author, we can use as an author. A second lesson outline follows. This is more suitable for students at an earlier stage of reading development and the focus is on reading, although there could be application to writing.

A Walk-Through of *The Birds at My Barn*

The front and back cover provide a panoramic view of the setting, mood, characters, topic, and theme of the first person recount. The child sitting at some distance from the barn studying a feather matches the reflective writing style within the book. The quiet colors reflect the gentle narration. Readers prepared for a thoughtful read are given another clue to reading style with the different birds on the front cover and the different feathers on the title page.

Pages 2 and 3

It is clear from the beginning that this is a first-person narrative. "My Barn" in the title is confirmed with "I went to our barn," so the child is on familiar territory. The thoughtful and comparative reading style is confirmed on the first double opening with the two similes—a sign from the author to slow down to consider detail. The introductory prepositional phrase of time, "early in the morning," sets the sentence and sequence pattern for the remainder of the book. The illustrations also reflect the natural rhythm of the day, increasing in brightness, and then becoming more subtle on the last pages.

Pages 4 and 5

"Early in the morning" has now become "In the cool morning." The thoughtful reading prompt is repeated here, but this time it is leading the reader to think beyond the text. Where did the birds go? The absence of text on page 5 could be an indication that readers need to do the wondering.

Pages 6 and 7

The amount of detail describing this incident is a model for inferential reading and thought. It is almost as if the author is saying, "Are we thinking in the same depth?" or perhaps, "Now you have the idea, let's go in more depth." Sentence length and structure is becoming more varied. Page 7 offers a different kind of introductory prepositional phrase of time. The green is greener, the day is moving on.

Pages 8 and 9

The similes have gone and the statements are presented more emphatically. There is more action. The language is moving up a notch, as in "dazzled me with flashes of brilliant blue."

Pages 10 and 11

I wonder how she got the paper bag, presumably her lunch. The verbs are the increased challenge on this page. They are becoming more specific. There is opportunity for inferential questioning or thinking on page 11 (Figure 17.1). Why was the crow scolding her? There is a change of perspective in the illustration, as the crow is above her.

He cawed down at me as I ate my lunch beneath his tree. I felt that he was scolding me with his "caw-caw-caw."

Figure 17.1: Page 11 from *The Birds at My Barn*

Pages 12 and 13

There is indication that the book is "winding down" with the lack of text on page 13. There are similarities with pages 4 and 5 in layout, and the rake seen on page 4 is here again. The transitional use of "as" as a sentence beginning on page 9 is included here within a sentence.

Pages 14 and 15

The color of the illustration reflects the day drawing to a close. The text is written as the author sees it, rather than being written in a way that allows the author to hope that the readers see it in the same way. It is almost as if the author has finished sharing her observations. But there is also an expectation that the narrator will be back for more tomorrow.

Page 16

The thought of more to come is reflected in the owl keeping watch. Once again, the author is encouraging the readers to think beyond the words. There is a lingering reflective feel to this ending.

A Lesson with Sixth-Grade Students

A sixth-grade teacher's musings:

> *I'm looking for something to encourage more detail in my students' personal writing. They include detail in expository text—they can get the information from another text but they don't seem to be able to draw it out of their own experience or knowledge. It is almost as if they think anything of their own is passé. The child in this book is younger than my students, but there's no condescension. In fact, it seems as if the character is really just the vehicle for the readers'*

thoughts. If I frame questions about the craft of the text rather than what it says I think it should work. The students know about, and are getting better at, thinking inferentially from a text. It just seems that they cannot translate to their own experiences through the pen. I am not sure if it would be better to read the book and then go to the park to observe birds or to think about using something else for their writing. Or, should they choose their topic and just focus on the detail. That's it. We'll read and discuss how the book hangs together and then what that means for our writing and then work from there. I wonder how many of the birds will be familiar? Probably not mourning doves. But that is at the end of the book, so that should be OK—they will be well into the text by then, so will cope with something in an easy book that isn't familiar. Sixth graders like to think they know everything.

The teacher used what she knew about her students and what she saw that the book offered to formulate the following questions, shown here in italics. Some of her thoughts and priorities are also included in parentheses.

Introducing the Book

What information does the cover provide that you think will help you think about how you might read this book?

What do you expect to be reading about?

(I need to make the distinction between the "what" and the "how." They will access the ideas between the type and style of book and the content.)

How does information help you think about your probable reading style?

(I want them to realize that even though it may appear to be an easy book, they will still need to read slowly and reflectively.)

What clue does the title page provide about your reading?

(Have they gotten the message about making comparisons?)

Reading the Book

Pages 2 and 3

How is the author indicating that she wants you to read slowly?

What other messages do the similes give about the way you might read and / or think about this book?

What do you notice about the color of the illustrations on these pages compared to those on the cover? What message is the illustrator conveying? OR In what ways do the illustrations reflect the text beyond the content?

Reread how this page is introduced. What does that lead you to expect as a transition to the next incident and text?

(I want to see if they pick up how the prepositional phrase of time provides the transitions and structure for the text, how it takes the story through the day. That is one aspect of detail I want to get them to think about in their writing.)

Pages 4 and 5

Had you made an accurate prediction about the way the text would start? What does that lead you to expect about the remainder of the book?

What reading beyond the text can you do on this page? What is the signal word to do that? Begin the next page in your head.

Pages 6 and 7

(I need to check that the students are beginning to understand just how much detail there is in the text and how the inferential thinking is supported.)

In what ways does the author's description of this incident differ from the previous two?

What did the author leave for you to contribute?

How is the author drawing you in so you feel as if you are either the "I" or a shadow of the narrator?

Think what you know about the shape of the text so far. What are you going to expect on the next page?

Pages 8 and 9

These two pages comprise one incident, yet they are two very different pages. Why do you think the author did that? To what effect?

Pages 10 and 11

What do you notice about the detail here?

What is the effect of the very specific verbs?

Think what time of day it is and think about where you are in the book. What do you expect to happen to the story line, to the text, and to the illustrations? Think of all three before you contribute any ideas to the group, as you will need to consider how they work together.

Pages 12 and 13

Which of your predictions could you confirm?

What is the author wanting you to compare this page with?

Pages 14 and 15

What happens to your thoughts and voice as you read this page? How did the author achieve that?

What has the author left you thinking about?

Page 16

Do you agree or do you not agree that no text is needed on this page? Justify your choice.

Following the Reading

Discuss learning about the birds, the techniques the author used to convey that information and to ensure the readers accessed the information, and which of the techniques the students might use in their writing. Discuss how transitional phrases add specificity to a recount. Students list the sequence of an experience, link these with transitional phrases, then add another layer of detail—perhaps similes, adverbial clauses, or one of other techniques from the book.

A Lesson With Younger Learners

The Birds at My Barn is also useful at earlier levels, as suggested by the leveling bar on the back of the book.

The teacher would need to know the features of the book in as much detail as outlined previously to be able to anticipate challenges and be ready to provide extra guidance.

The questions shown in italics below do not constitute a complete lesson. The teacher needs to be responsive to the decoding strategies the students use and, when necessary, prompt or provoke the application of those most appropriate.

Introducing the Book

When you see the word "my" in the title, what are some words you expect to meet in the text?

Open the book so you can see both covers. What else do the covers tell you about the book?

Have you thought about where it happens, the time of day, why the birds might come to the barn?

We know what the book will tell us about. How might the author tell us that? Do you expect this to be a story or a letter or a poem or a text that tells us how to find birds? Open the book at any page and read with your eyes to confirm or change your thoughts about how the author will tells about the birds.

What did you notice?

What do you notice about the illustration on the title page? If they are different feathers, what does that tell us about the birds and what we might need to do as we read?

Pages 2 and 3—Figure 17.2

Read these pages with your eyes. (Time should be given at each page turning to reread the previous page and to read the next text before being asked to read orally or to answer questions.)

What did you find out?

Which words told you when? What do we call it when we have a group of words like that?

How did the author describe the nest? What else did she describe with a simile?

I wonder why the author did not just say, "The eggs were in the nest." How much more do we know?

Read these two pages again and then turn to the next two pages.

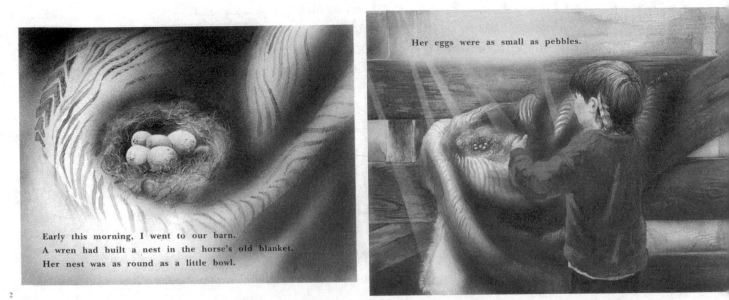

Early this morning, I went to our barn.
A wren had built a nest in the horse's old blanket.
Her nest was as round as a little bowl.

Her eggs were as small as pebbles.

Figure 17.2: Pages 2 and 3 of *The Birds at My Barn*

Pages 4 and 5

What do you notice about the beginning phrase of words?

What does that lead you to expect on the next page?

What word has the author used instead of the word "thinking"? If we changed the "w" to a "p," then what word would we have made? Would it have still made sense if the author had used that word? (I often write ideas such as this and the response to the next question on Post-It® notes, and then attach them to the appropriate page. At the end of the lesson we have a reference for discussion points, and then the notes are left on the inside front or back cover for students to refer to or place on the correct page on subsequent independent readings.)

What did the author leave you to add about the wren and her mate? How could you write that?

Pages 6 and 7

What do we now know about the pattern the author is using to tell us about the birds at the barn?

Which word on this page has a similar meaning to "wondered" and "pondered"?

Which word tells how the flags moved?

Notice the second sentence on page 7. That is a long sentence without any extra punctuation. Read it in your head again to see which words go together and where you could pause.

What kind of grain might it be?

Pages 8 and 9

I wonder why the colors in the illustrations are becoming so bright.

Which words in the text describe color or what bright color does?

There are not many words that have a double "Z" in them. Can you think of another one? Let's just write a couple now and come back to add more later.

What word on page 9 has something in common with the word "flew"?

Pages 10 and 11

What could the author have said instead of "noon"? Can you think of more than one way?

Find the verbs—the words that tell what the crow did or was doing. How would you describe what the author wanted you to think about each one?

What made the girl think the crow was angry with her?

Do you think he really was angry or scolding her?

Pages 12 and 13

The author is using some compound words. We had "leftover" earlier and we have two on this page. Which are they?

The second sentence is another long one. Think back to how you knew when to pause last time. Try that again. Now read the sentence aloud.

Find two words on this page for which you could suggest other words the author could have used.

Pages 14 and 15

These are the last pages of text. What does the author need to do?

There is another long sentence for you to decide when to pause.

What is the author leaving you to think about?

Page 16

Why was the owl a good choice of illustration for the last page?

Now it is late in the day, and the sun is setting behind the oak trees.
All around me the mourning doves are cooing as the day gently comes to a close.

15

Figure 17.3: Page 15 of *The Birds at My Barn*

Conclusion

The Present's Presence

Every present provokes thought and emotions within the giver and the receiver. The giver has made a conscious choice, thinking about the recipient, wondering how it will be received and if the present will be useful. The recipient thinks about the giver and considers where to put the present and how and when it could be used or admired. Whatever the motive for the present may have been, it changes both the giver and the receiver in some way. Each have either confirmed or amended understandings about their relationship through the selection and receiving of the present, which in itself is a manifestation of unseen, and perhaps unspoken, thoughts about the other person. The present is a signal for a celebratory exchange of thoughts. There's spoken and unspoken dialogue.

And so it is with a book. Every reading or piece of writing initiates spoken and/or unspoken dialogue and changes both the reader and the writer. Engagement in the creation or recreation of a text confirms or amends our understandings and behaviors in some way. As a result of what we read we either confirm or change our knowledge about the topic, our understandings about the underlying theme of the work, or our opinions about the issue. As a result of how we read, we either confirm or change our knowledge of and understandings about how words work, how books and texts work, and how language works. And so our confidence and competence as readers and writers is confirmed or amended. When we consider that this applies to every reading within a classroom, the selection of texts of the highest quality possible becomes paramount. If our students are to enjoy and savor the benefits of reading and writing, nothing less than the very best will do—either in the material or the way it is presented. There can be no kidding, no pretension of any kind.

The new-but-now-tattered book fell out of Jamie's book bag. I managed to restrain a gasp, but the mother, sensing my reaction, offered, "Yes, I'm afraid it is a bit the worse for wear. Almost loved to bits, in fact. He's read the words off the page." He picked up the book and looked up at me appealingly. "Can I take it home tonight? I'm not quite finished with it yet."

A present indeed!

Bibliography

References

Duke, Nell. 2000. "3.6 Minutes per Day: The Scarcity of Informational Texts in First Grade." *Reading Research Quarterly*, Volume 35, issue 2, April–June, 202–224.

Meek, Margaret. 1982. *Learning to Read*. London: The Bodley Head, 20–21.

Mooney, Margaret E. 2001. *Text Forms and Features: A Resource for Intentional Teaching*. Katonah, NY: Richard C. Owen Publishers, Inc.

The Chicago Manual of Style: The 13th Edition of a Manual of Style Revised and Extended. 1998. Chicago, IL: The University of Chicago Press.

Materials Cited

Allen, Casey Lynn. 2000. *And Then There Were Birds* from Books for Young Learners Collection. Katonah, NY: Richard C. Owen Publishers, Inc.

Anderson, Barbara. 1996. *Proud Garments*. Wellington, New Zealand: Victoria University Press.

Boland, Janice. 1997. *The Pond* from Books for Young Learners Collection. Katonah, NY: Richard C. Owen Publishers, Inc.

Books for Young Learners Collection published by Richard C. Owen Publishers, Inc., Katonah, NY, 1995 to present.

Brontë, Charlotte. 2003. *Jane Eyre*. New York: Dover Publications. Originally published in 1847.

Cooper, Sarah Katz. 2002. *Search and Discover.* Newbridge Discovery Links. New York: Newbridge.

Cowley, Joy. 1983. *Greedy Cat* from Ready to Read Collection. Wellington, New Zealand: Learning Media Ltd (then School Publications).

Cox, Rhonda. 1997. *Chickens* from Books for Young Learners Collection. Katonah, NY: Richard C. Owen Publishers, Inc.

Cox, Rhonda. 1996. *Pigs Peek* from Books for Young Learners Collection. Katonah, NY: Richard C. Owen Publishers, Inc.

Cox, Rhonda. 2000. *Watermelon* from Books for Young Learners Collection. Katonah, NY: Richard C. Owen Publishers, Inc.

Crowe, Andrew. 1992. *Which Native Tree?* Auckland, New Zealand: Penguin Books.

Danzer, Gerald A. et al. 2003. *The Americans.* Evanston, IL: McDougal Littell.

Degen, Bruce. 1995. *Jamberry.* New York: Harper Festival.

Frost, Robert. 1969. "Blue-Butterfly Day" in *The Poetry of Robert Frost.* New York: Henry Holt and Company. First published in *The New Republic,* 1921.

Jackson, Carolyn. 2002. *Hometowns,* Discovery Links. New York: Newbridge.

Jackson, Marjorie. 2002. *A Family of Beavers* from Books for Young Learners Collection. Katonah, NY: Richard C. Owen Publishers, Inc.

Lee, Frances. 1999. *Too Many Animals* from Alphakids. St Leonards, Australia: Horwitz Martin.

Lewis, C. S. 1998. *The Lion, the Witch and the Wardrobe.* Hammersmith, London: HarperCollins. Originally published in 1950.

Marcus, Ellen. 2002. *Raving about Rainforests* from News Extra Collection. St Leonards, Australia: Horwitz Education. Distributed in the United States by Richard C. Owen Publishers, Inc.

Martin Jr, Bill. 1992. *Brown Bear, Brown Bear, What Do You See?* New York: Holt.

Martin, Rafe. 1992. *A Storyteller's Story* from the Meet the Author Collection. Katonah, NY: Richard C. Owen Publishers, Inc.

McPherson, Jan. 1998. "Dear Red Riding Hood" in *Junior Journal 19.* Wellington, New Zealand: Learning Media for Ministry of Education.

Miller, Kenneth R. and Joseph Levine. 2002. *Biology*. New Jersey: Prentice Hall.

Moeller, Kathleen Hardcastle. 2000. *The Birds at My Barn* from Books for Young Learners Collection. Katonah, NY: Richard C. Owen Publishers, Inc. A copy of this title is included with this book.

Moeller, Kathleen Hardcastle. 1998. *Hoketichee and the Manatee* from Book for Young Learners Collection. Katonah, NY: Richard C. Owen Publishers, Inc.

Mooney, Margaret. 2000. *The Busy Harvest* from Newbridge Discovery Links. New York, NY: Newbridge Educational Publishing.

Morse, Steven. 2001. *Cool* from Books for Young Learners Collection. Katonah, NY: Richard C. Owen Publishers, Inc.

Opat, Debbie. 2000. *Minibeasts* from The News Collection. St Leonards, New South Wales, Australia: Horwitz Education. A copy of this title is included with this book.

Potter, Beatrix. 1902. *The Tale of Peter Rabbit*. London: Frederick Warne.

Rowling, J. K. 1997. *Harry Potter and the Philosopher's Stone*. London: Bloomsbury Publishing Plc.

Shahan, Sherry. 1997. *The Hungry Sea Star* from Books for Young Learners Collection. Katonah, NY: Richard C. Owen Publishers, Inc.

Silvano, Wendi J. 2000. *Pancakes for Breakfast* from Books for Young Learners Collection. Katonah, NY: Richard C. Owen Publishers, Inc.

Tennyson, Lord Alfred. 1864. "The Charge of the Light Brigade."

2004 Catalog from Richard C. Owen Publishers, Inc.

Index

A book
is a present
you give
yourself
every time
you open it.